Items should be returned on or before the last date shown below. Items not already requested by other borrowers may be renewed in person, in writing or by telephone. To renew, please quote the number on the barcode label. To renew online a PIN is required. This can be requested at your local library.
Renew online @ **www.dublincitypubliclibraries.ie**
Fines charged for overdue items will include postage incurred in recovery. Damage to or loss of items will be charged to the borrower. 822/LYN

Leabharlanna Poiblí Chathair Bhaile Átha Cliath
Dublin City Public Libraries

Dublin City
Baile Átha Cliath

Brainse Dhromchonnrach
Drumcondra Branch
Tel. 8377206

Date Due	Date Due	Date Due
1 8 AUG 2015		
1 0 APR 2018		

LAY UP YOUR ENDS

LAY UP YOUR ENDS
A Twenty-Fifth Anniversary Edition

MARTIN LYNCH
& THE CHARABANC
THEATRE COMPANY

edited by Richard Palmer
with an introduction by Brenda Winter

LAGAN PRESS
BELFAST
2008

For the rights (amateur only) to performance of this play, contact:
Drama League of Ireland, The Mill Theatre, Dundrum Town Centre,
Dundrum, Dublin 16, Republic of Ireland. e-mail: dli@eircom.net

Published by
Lagan Press
1A Bryson Street
Belfast BT5 4ES
e-mail: lagan-press@e-books.org.uk
web: lagan-press.org.uk

ISBN: 978 1 904652 49 6

Author: Martin Lynch
and the Charabanc Theatre Company
Title: Lay Up Your Ends:
A Twenty-Fifth Anniversary Edition
2008

Set in Palatino
Printed by J.H. Haynes, Sparkford

Acknowledgements

I wish to convey my thanks for their help in this publication to: Brenda Winter for her considered and highly illuminating introduction; Marie Jones, Martin Lynch, Carol Moore, Ian McElhinney and Cherrie McIlwaine for the contributions they have written especially for this edition; Paul Hadfield, Gerry Colgan and Fionnuala O'Connor for giving permission to reproduce 'Nothing Run of the Mill', '*Lay Up Your Ends* at the John Player' and 'Theatre from the Mills' respectively; the *Irish News* for permission to reproduce 'Kitty's Memories Inspire New Play' and 'The Lynch Scalpel Leaves Them in Stitches'; the *Belfast News Letter*, *Belfast Telegraph*, *Guardian* and *Sovetskaya Kultura* for permission to reprint 'Impressive Women', 'Dramatic View of Life in the Mill', 'The Past Run Through the Mill' and 'The Amazons from Belfast' respectively; John Killen, Yvonne Murphy and Ross Moore of the Linenhall Library, Belfast, for their assistance in accessing material in the library's Theatre Archive and Hugh Odling-Smee (formerly the Theatre Archivist) for his help in accessing the original script; all those who have given me access to their personal archives; Louis Edmondson and John O'Hara for permission to reproduce their photographs of the Russian Tour and finally, but by no means least, those at the Lagan Press for their suggestions, advice and patience.

Richard Palmer

Photographic acknowledgements

The publishers would like to acknowledge the kind permission of the following photographers whose work appears in the photographic section of this book. We would also like to thank those individuals who offered prints from their own personal collections. Finally, we would like to record our appreciation of the staff in charge of the Theatre and Performing Arts Archive at the Linen Hall Library, Belfast, for their help and assistance.

Page 2, top: John O'Hara *(Personal collection of Brenda Winter)*

Page 2, bottom: John O'Hara *(Linen Hall Library, Belfast)*

Page 3: Chris Hill Photography *(Theatre Archive, Linen Hall Library, Belfast)*

Page 4, top: John O'Hara *(Personal collection of Brenda Winter)*

Page 4, bottom: Chris Hill Photography *(Linen Hall Library, Belfast)*

Page 5: Chris Hill Photography *(Personal collection of Carol Moore)*

Page 6: Chris Hill Photography *(Personal collection of Brenda Winter)*

Page 7, top photo: John O'Hara *(Personal collection of Carol Moore)*

Page 7, bottom: John O'Hara *(Linen Hall Library, Belfast)*

Page 8: John O'Hara *(Personal collection of Carol Moore)*

Page 9: John O'Hara *(Personal collection of Carol Moore)*

Page 10, both: from the collection of Cherrie McIlwaine

Page 11, top: from the collection of Carol Moore

Page 11, bottom: Louis Edmondson

Page 12: Storyline of *Lay Up Your Ends* *(Personal collection of Carol Moore)*

Page 13, both: from the collection of Carol Moore

Page 14: top: John O'Hara

Page 14, bottom: Louis Edmondson

Page 15, top: John O'Hara

Page 15, bottom: Louis Edmondson

for Sadie Patterson
and all those who still labour for social justice

Contents

Biographical Notes

'That's Not Theatre, Love!'

The Lay Up Your Ends *Experience*

It has taken twenty-five years for the theatrical phenomenon that was *Lay Up Your Ends* to make its way into print. For reasons of copyright this play, Charabanc's first production, had to be omitted from Claudia Harris's anthology of four early Charabanc plays published in 2006.[1] This omission represented a considerable drawback to an understanding of how this play, in many ways the company's central text, shaped and influenced Charabanc's subsequent engagement with popular theatre forms.

In its twelve-year existence Charabanc brought working-class women and men into theatres. It generated a huge amount of new writing demonstrating that women could produce work which was funny and meaningful and relevant to people's lives. It is credited with being 'in the vanguard of independent touring in Ireland'[2] inspiring the plethora of younger companies which followed in its wake. A study of the company's tattered scrapbook[3] reveals that, from London to Leningrad and from the Baltic to Baltimore, they were praised

for their 'pithy and dark and incisively unsentimental humour
... and their ensemble playing'. The seeds of all of this
achievement were sown in the upsurge of collective initiative
and creative energy which generated *Lay Up Your Ends*.

The impact of the company in its time and its significance in
the development of Irish theatre have never been fully
recognised. *The Cambridge Companion to Twentieth-Century Irish
Drama*, one of the most recent publications in the field of Irish
theatre studies, almost occludes Charabanc. Brief accounts of
the history of Charabanc are to be found in other modern
overviews of Irish theatre though reference is usually confined
to a few obligatory paragraphs in the one obligatory chapter
given over to consideration of theatre in the north of the
country. Often Charabanc's work is ghettoised as community
or women's theatre, never part of the mainstream and
definitely not canonical. Of course all of this could be
attributed to the fact that the work was simply not worthy of
further comment or evaluation. Or it could be, as the American
scholar Helen Lojek has suggested, that some theatre scholars
hold firmly to the opinion that 'accessible works cannot be
serious; [and that] popular culture, not needing explanation, is
[consequently] devalued'.[4]

Ophelia Byrne's more extensive and enthusiastic
consideration of the contribution of Charabanc to Northern
Irish theatre focuses on the gender of the founders and their
unemployed status. She identifies them on two counts as being
of the peripheral groups of 'women' and the 'unemployed'[5]
who are 'rigorously opposed and excluded at a social level'.[6]
This exclusion is well-illustrated by a description of the
position and status of women on the island of Ireland at the
time when *Lay Up Your Ends* was in gestation.

In the Irish Republic of the late 1970s 'women held only 7

per cent of senior positions in the civil service and local authorities'; the Irish Dail boasted only five women TDs and there were 'no women in the High Court and Supreme Court'; 'only a handful of women [were] on the boards of the 100 top public companies in Ireland [and] there was still a handful of pubs in Dublin that would not serve women in the bar'.[7] Across the border in Northern Ireland the situation for women was not very different. Entrenched attitudes towards the home as the only place 'where a woman's influence is socially acceptable'[8] resulted in Northern Ireland becoming a late-developer in terms of equal opportunity for women. The distracting effect of thirty years of sectarian violence had also pushed feminist concerns way down the political agenda. The perception that women had no place in the public sphere is reflected in the experiences of Brenda Winter and Marie Jones who recall how, in the course of their research for *Lay Up Your Ends*, they interviewed the managing director of a prominent Belfast linen firm. However, although the women asked the questions, the manager's answers were directed to their male producer, Ian McElhinney.[9]

As actors in Belfast in the early 1980s the female founders of Charabanc were employed, or rather mostly unemployed, in an industry where 'women were proportionately under-represented in the most senior directorial posts ... and in the membership of theatre boards'.[10] In Belfast 'the three main houses, the Grand Opera House, the Belfast Civic Arts Theatre and the Lyric Players Theatre, were controlled by male boards of directors'.[11] An examination of the Lyric's cast-lists between August 1981 and July 1982 reveals that in that year eighty-three male and thirty-eight female roles were cast in a season which exclusively featured the work of male playwrights. Casting decisions were the responsibility of the Lyric's new artistic director, Leon Rubin, who exacerbated an already bad employment situation by 'importing' actors from England to play leading roles in the season. The employment prospects for actresses living and working in Belfast at this time were truly dire. It was indignation that galvanised the founders of Charabanc into doing something about their disempowered situation.

The idea to form a community theatre company did not spring ready-formed from the brains of the Charabanc actresses. Rather it was a series of local influences—from individuals and from other companies—which led them to take this action. The first of these influences was Playzone Community Theatre[12] which was in many ways the precursor of Charabanc.

Playzone is a company which is occluded from studies of theatre in Northern Ireland. Yet it was the Playzone model which allowed the Charabanc actresses to recognize that it was possible to tour theatre to community centres. A similarity in style of playing and choice of subject-matter which 'sought to be popular'[13] drew comparisons between the two companies from the theatre critic of the *News Letter*. In his review of the first performance of *Lay up Your Ends* he commented: 'It owes much to the now defunct Playzone concept of which Sarah [Marie] Jones was a part'.[14] Jones and indeed Stephen Rea, co-founder of Field Day, had been Playzone company members.

Until Playzone was founded Northern Ireland had remained virtually untouched by the alternative and community theatre movement which was flourishing in Great Britain during the seventies. In 1977 Belfast was served by the Lyric Players and the Ulster Actors' Company at the Arts Theatre. The 1977-78 roster of productions at the Lyric was largely made up of Irish, European and American classics with the stage nudity of Peter

Shaffer's *Equus* providing the only frisson of controversy.[15] The Arts Theatre 'fulfilled its brief, with productions ranging from popular comedies to children's entertainment, variety and classics'.[16] The tiny Group Theatre was home to a thriving amateur drama movement and Interplay provided a theatre-in-education service to schools.[17] Theatre touring to the regions was confined to 'buy-ins' such as Theatre North which was based in England and the Irish Theatre Company based in the Republic of Ireland.[18] Imelda Foley, then working in Derry as a Regional Development Officer, highlighted the paucity of indigenous professional theatrical activity at the time in Northern Ireland outside Belfast, likening herself and her fellow officer, Bill Collins, to 'cowboys in the Wild West'.[19] However, as the seventies progressed the notion that theatre could emerge from and serve the needs of the grassroots was presenting 'a challenge to the state's cultural engineers'[20] in the Arts Council of Northern Ireland.

7:84, Red Ladder, Monstrous Regiment of Women and Joint Stock[21] were among myriad British companies springing up during the sixties and seventies who concerned themselves with 'the contribution theatre practice can make to the welfare of the community'.[22] Many of these companies, most importantly 7:84, were politically oppositional to what they perceived to be the oppressive policies of the state and sought to uncover and challenge the ideological hegemony of the middle classes as a means of effecting social and political change. Prior to the advent of the alternative and community theatre movement in Britain in the sixties, theatre was considered by working-class people to be the preserve of the middle classes and to have nothing to do with their lives. British alternative theatre sought to challenge these perceptions. To do so they took plays out of theatre buildings and into the familiar surroundings of the community. Audiences, however, 'did not come ready-made'[23] and companies had to work hard to woo new community audiences with material which reflected their lives and concerns.

In the mid-seventies 'following the lead given by cultural critics such as Richard Hoggart and Raymond Williams' there was a swing in Arts Council funding priorities 'Towards Cultural Democracy'.[24] This shift in policy gradually began to filter through to the Arts Council of Northern Ireland who in 1978 would designate Community Arts as a discrete area for funding purposes.[25] Playzone's intentions were completely in tune with the new requirements for a more equitable disbursement of funds to develop theatre projects in both regional and deprived urban areas and subsidy was subsequently secured. Playzone toured to schools, retirement homes (with a reminiscence project) and working-men's clubs. The company was in existence for barely two years before collapsing in debt. Marie Jones was with the company from its inception to its demise and she experienced at first hand with Playzone how the aesthetics of a theatre performance must reflect and be influenced by the culture of the community to which it is playing. Playzone prefigured and influenced Charabanc by its position and politics as 'a theatre of social engagement—committed to bringing about change in specific communities'.[26] Playzone, however, did not devise work, relying primarily on existing scripts, nor did it have in the range of its activities as clear a political focus as did Charabanc who found its *raison d'être* in foregrounding the experience of Belfast working-class women.

Of equal significance to the formation of Charabanc was the impact of the opening night of Martin Lynch's play *Dockers* at the Lyric Theatre. Lynch, born and reared in the rough and tumble of the docks area of Belfast, is a political activist turned playwright. His working-class background had afforded him little exposure to or experience of theatre. Whilst working as an administrator for the Republican Clubs Organisation (now renamed the Workers' Party) he 'had been set the task of finding venues for John Arden's *The Non-Stop Connolly Show*'[27] when it came to Belfast in 1976. The impact of witnessing this performance by one of Britain's earliest proponents of community theatre made Lynch, a committed socialist, realise the efficacy of theatre in the 'wider political struggle for the right of a people or section of a society to control its own identity'.[28] Inspired by what he felt to be the potency of this new tool for the politicisation of the working class, he set about writing plays and forming his own company. His work with the Turf Lodge Fellowship Community Theatre, named after the area where he was then living, concerned itself with highlighting the experience of working-class people whose lives would otherwise go unnoticed and unrecorded. By 1980 he had come to the attention of the Lyric Theatre who believed that in Lynch they had found the 'Northern Irish O'Casey'.[29] He was appointed writer-in-residence and on the 13th January 1981 his first play, *Dockers*[30], opened at the Lyric Theatre.

The effect of this play on those of the Charabanc actresses present for the première was dramatic. Roy Connolly has described the first night of *Dockers* when Lynch bussed in dock-workers and their families to authenticate, by their presence, the performance of a popular, working-class drama in the middle-class setting of the Lyric Theatre.[31] If the dockers felt empowered by witnessing their lives enacted on the stage, the local actors felt equally validated through hearing their own accent, idiom and cultural identity revitalised on the stage of the Lyric Theatre. Lynch's employment of local popular culture was novel and effective. The Charabanc actresses were exhilarated by what they witnessed and encouraged by the rapturous reception which the play received.[32] Lynch had shown the way and the Charabanc actresses, though they didn't articulate it at the time, were inspired to create similar work for themselves.

It took nearly two years before it became clear how this task would be accomplished. In the interim period they continued to work when and how they could. Casting policies at the Lyric had not only 'engendered' unemployment and resentment but a number of profit-sharing initiatives such as Belfast Theatre Company and New Writers' Theatre. These companies provided some creative substance but the difficulties inherent in running a theatre company without any financial resources made for a constant struggle and profit-sharing initiatives were usually short-lived. Spurred on by frustration the local theatre community formed the Belfast Actors' Centre in 1982 to provide training workshops to improve core skills such as voice, movement, stage-fighting and musical theatre.[33] They pooled their own expertise and persuaded sympathetic visiting actors to contribute to the venture. All of the Charabanc actresses were key players in this enterprise which briefly united Belfast actors in collective self-help. However, to hone skills for employment opportunities which rarely materialise, inevitably leads to even more frustration and the Belfast Actors' Centre became another victim of malaise and discontent. However, their involvement in its organisation provided the Charabanc actresses with valuable experience of what could be achieved through common purpose and collective action.

It is not clear who came up with the idea that a project reflecting women's issues should be embarked upon or when precisely these particular women decided to band together. What is documented is that in November 1982 four of the five Charabanc actresses were employed in the Belfast Civic Arts Theatre production of the children's show, *The World of Hans Christian Andersen*.[34] Even though appearing in 'the kids' B-show' in the less prestigious of the two producing houses in Belfast was considered fairly menial employment, the actresses were grateful to be in work over the Christmas period and dreaded the inevitability of the dole queue once the strains of 'Wonderful, Wonderful Copenhagen' faded into the distance in January. Eleanor Methven is on record as stating that Charabanc gave her 'the opportunity to play more interesting roles than a succession of Norahs and Cathleens.'[35] In *The World of Hans Christian Andersen* Moore (Scanlan), Winter, Jones and Macauley were only too thankful to have the opportunity to play assorted witches, dogs, mermaids, tin soldiers and most memorably the prow of a boat! It was during this period that they decided to approach Martin Lynch to ask him to write some sketches which they could tour round community centres. They experienced no sense of irony in the fact that they were five women approaching a man to write material on women's issues. Lynch put them right by insisting they write the material themselves.

They had started their 'job creation scheme' with the vague notion of doing a project which reflected their own identity as Belfast women. They decided that their own experience 'could not be viewed in isolation from the history of [their] own mothers and grandmothers'. It was their experience which had 'made the women of today'.[36] The starting point for research was the newspaper collection at Belfast Central Library where they first read of the 1911 Belfast mill-girls' strike. The dramatic potential of this subject interested the actresses and at their next regular Sunday evening meeting with Lynch, it was decided that they should commence a process of oral research amongst former textile workers. Interviews were not difficult to facilitate. Linen, along with ship-building and rope, had been central to the prosperity of Belfast since the Industrial Revolution. In the fifties and sixties the linen industry had effectively been decimated by the introduction of man-made fibres but in 1982 there were still plenty of old mill-girls in Belfast who had started and ended their working lives in the mills. Inspired by the writings of folklorist Betty Messenger, who had conducted research amongst mill-girls in the seventies,[37] the actresses set about recording interviews with mill-workers in their own homes. They heard tales of hazardous working conditions, punitive terms and conditions of employment and lives dominated by poverty and privation.

The impact of their findings was of vital importance in the politicisation of the Charabanc actresses. Outraged by the mill-workers' descriptions of hardship and oppression, the original Charabanc aesthetic became infused with political intent. Of particular significance was an interview with the veteran trade union organiser Sadie Patterson. This meeting was seminal in motivating the women of Charabanc to tell the story of the 1911 mill-girls' strike. There is no doubt that the actresses equated their own sense of powerlessness with that of their subjects. Although they most certainly did not endure the grinding poverty or physical deprivations of the mill-women, they certainly did share their marginality and invisibility as women. In his 1984 review of *Lay Up Your Ends* at the Drill Hall [London], Peter Hepple seems to have merged the identities of the five Charabanc actresses with the mill-women they were portraying:

> There is a joy in seeing these women really being their forbears, made aware of the benefits of organising themselves against an ignorant and narrow-minded employer, finding delight in a new kind of companionship, slightly amazed at their courage in standing up for what they believe in.[38]

Hepple had cannily put his finger on the 'engine' that fuelled these performances: the shared experience of the modern-day actresses and the historical mill-girls; their lack of agency and their empowerment through organisation and collective action.

Charabanc was now seeking, whether they consciously realised it or not, to create a piece of political theatre. They knew what they wanted to do and why they wanted to do it but without a director who was also a good script-editor they were, as yet, unsure how to set about crafting the scenes they had devised with Lynch into a play. At the time there were no directors in Belfast with the experience necessary to negotiate the difficulties inherent in a piece of theatre which had been written collaboratively. The actresses also felt strongly that they wanted a woman to direct them. Lynch had met the English director Pam Brighton at the Edinburgh Festival in August 1982 where she had been directing Peter Sheridan's play, *Diary of a Hunger Striker*, for Hull Truck Theatre Company. Lynch and Brighton were each impressed with the commitment of the other towards using theatre as a means to further radical socialist politics. They were both violently opposed to Thatcher's 'sweeping privatisation of previously nationalised industries, total decimation of other industries [and] the corollary rise in unemployment'.[39] Brighton had directed for The Royal Court London, 7:84, Monstrous Regiment of Women, Hull Truck, the Half Moon Theatre and the Liverpool Everyman where she had been instrumental in developing the work of Willy Russell. Lynch invited her to come to Belfast to direct *Lay Up Your Ends*. Brighton was always attracted to the unconventional in her choice of work and could not resist the opportunity to come to the rescue of five out-of-work women in 'war-torn' Belfast.

An experienced director and script-editor, Brighton was immediately tasked with forming the scenes which had been written into a cohesive drama. A veteran in devising theatre, she soon imposed a routine. A scene would be discussed by the whole group and revisions agreed upon. Either Jones or Lynch would then take the scene away to rewrite, usually overnight. The scene would then be returned to the group for further discussion and further revision if it was thought necessary. The constant discussion and revision was a tortuous and unwieldy experience. Brighton later commented that 'the working process of Charabanc [felt] like someone newly delivered of quads— how to deal with it in the confines of normal spaces'.[40] The process could, and did, continue right into performance. Jones in 1987 commented: 'Because we're writing our own stuff, it's never finished. We're always striving to make it better—to perfect it. It's a good opportunity that actors don't normally get'.[41] The endless process of research, writing, discussion and revision did give each actress the opportunity to make an intellectual, creative and emotional contribution to the character she was to play. The writers were then able to write specifically for each individual and constantly to 'tailor' the character so that it fitted the actress like another skin. All of these factors contributed to 'the extraordinary vibrancy of characterisation'[42] so frequently highlighted in critical reception.

Lay Up Your Ends, the story of the 1911 Belfast mill-girls' strike, opened on 15th May 1983 at the Arts Theatre, Belfast.

The audiences who attended the première came in expectation of seeing something which was meaningful to their community. Interest in Charabanc's project had been whipped up by Martin Lynch's weekly column in the *Irish News*.[43] Speculation and curiosity had also been generated by the research process itself. Although they were aware that news was spreading about their theatrical activities, nothing could have prepared the company for 'the queues stretching from the Arts Theatre [down] the whole length of Botanic Avenue clamouring for admission'.[44] There was 'a packed-to-bursting house'. Foremost amongst the crowd and listed first under acknowledgements in the programme, were the former mill-girls who had helped with the research.[45] The event had all the atmosphere of a spontaneous, haphazard, community event put together on a shoestring budget. The hierarchies of the great and the good familiar at most theatre 'first nights' were just not present at the opening of *Lay Up Your Ends*. Only local critics were in attendance. No-one came from Dublin or London to review. Interest in Charabanc from these quarters came only when news spread about the spectacular success of the first performance. The audience reaction to the performance was vociferous and beyond appreciation. The Northern Ireland politician Paddy Devlin who was present that evening, subsequently recorded:

> I was uplifted that night ... even yet I feel still as emotionally involved. For the feeling lingers not so much about the performance I saw on stage as from the inspiration that five young actresses created for the rest of us to get off our asses and do something for ourselves and our community.[46]

Charabanc had entered into true 'communitas'[47] with its Belfast audience. The love affair was to continue the following night when it embarked upon its real *raison d'être*: a tour of community venues. They received a rapturous reception in St Agnes' Parish Hall in Catholic West Belfast and, being no respecters of sectarian divides, played a subsequent night at the Stadium Leisure Centre in the Protestant Shankill district. By October *Lay Up Your Ends* had toured extensively to community centres, leisure centres, converted cinemas and theatre venues, in rural and urban areas, north and south of the border. The company then played to acclaim at the Dublin Theatre Festival and at the Glasgow Mayfest where they won the prestigious 'Spirit of the Festival' award. A tour of the then Soviet Union in November 1984 took the company to Moscow, Leningrad (now St Petersburg) and Vilnius in Lithuania. This 'legendary' expedition was followed by a London run of the play.

In July 1983 Charabanc Theatre Company brought *Lay Up Your Ends* to the Flax Trust Community Centre in the Ardoyne area of north Belfast. The building had formerly been a spinning mill. The 'site-specific' resonances of the occasion created an additional dimension to the evening's performance for both actors and audience. Rosalind Carne writing for the Guardian noted an 'excitement of recognition'[48] in the play's reception. This reaction was not surprising as the audience on that night included a substantial number of former textile workers. After the show one of the women approached Marie Jones, grabbed her by the arm and whispered, 'That's not theatre, love! Sure anybody would enjoy that'.[49] The woman was identifying herself as the 'anybody' who might feel excluded, or who might exclude herself, from going to the theatre. She did not equate what she had just seen with her perception of a play as a 'high art' cultural form alien to her experience as an 'ordinary' working-class person. Encoded in this simple yet profound response is the reason why

Charabanc enjoyed such popular success at grassroots level and, conversely, why its work has generated comparatively little critical attention in the field of Irish theatre studies.

In its critical reception *Lay Up Your Ends* provoked both positive and negative responses. The play puzzled some theatre-goers. Though commonplace now, the minimalist, non-illusionist *mise-en-scène* in which people changed character in full-view by donning a hat or shawl was new to Irish audiences. Most disturbingly of all, the female performers transgressed the boundaries of sexual difference by putting on items of male clothing to transform themselves into the mill-workers' husbands. In this way they were enabled to hold up to ridicule the men's attitude to their women as misogynistic, oppressive and erroneous. In *Lay Up Your Ends* the audience was also able to witness, through the portrayal of the ruthless and conniving mill boss (Eric Bingham) by a cross-dressed actress, 'that a woman can have political power and feel emotions otherwise considered the prerogative of men'.[50] It has to be said that the decision to cross-dress, though enriching in its result, was taken for purely pragmatic reasons: the company could not find a male actor in Belfast who fulfilled the criteria of the government job-creation scheme which was funding company wages. Not one male actor had been out of work for over six months.

On the first night of *Lay Up Your Ends* the reviewer from the *Belfast News Letter* was impressed by this new type of theatre that he had witnessed but seemed unsure how to categorise the play, calling it 'a chronicle' rather than a drama.[51] He was unable to fit the play into any recognisable matrix of Irish literary drama. Only the theatre cognoscenti present that night would have realised that Charabanc were engaging with methodologies from British popular, political theatre practice of the 1960s and 70s not previously employed in this way on the stage in Northern Ireland. Introduced to these methods by Pam Brighton, Charabanc had engaged immediately with this alternative form of theatre, recognising its potential to bear witness to the inequitable treatment of the working-class women who toiled in the linen mills of Belfast.

Helen Lojek has commented that

> ... it is one sign of the isolation of theatre in Belfast and the relative naïveté of Charabanc's founding members that they seem to have been unaware of such companies as England's Woman's Theatre Group and Monstrous Regiment of Women, which would have provided clear models for their own efforts.[52]

It was, however, probably fortuitous that Charabanc did not model itself slavishly on any existing company, Irish or British, but rather chose like the Ulster Literary Theatre before them to make their 'own way of things'.[53] They responded to the practices of British Theatre methodology on an instinctive level and adjusted and adapted its techniques until they created a way of working which came to be recognised as a distinctive 'Charabanc style' of performance. Their primary concern was to create a piece of theatre which was enjoyable and through which the political message could be conveyed. By putting the 'theatre' first they managed to avoid many of the difficulties encountered by their more ideology-driven British counterparts, many of whom used theatre methods as a means to promote their 'socialist or Marxist philosophies'.[54] A Red Ladder programme note from 1972 reads: 'Theatre is not our end; it is our means ... a means of stimulating thought, discussion and even action, on issues of critical importance to the working class'.[55] In their quest for anti-hierarchical company structures and 'non-oppressive' working practices many British companies turned to a collaborative means of production wherein each performer would have equal responsibility for producing the script. This approach often resulted in 'a total decentralisation, a total exchange of roles. Everybody was a writer; everybody was a bureaucrat; everybody could do anything on the show. It was total chaos.'[56]

The Charabanc actresses had also agreed to a collaborative approach with everyone contributing research and ideas. However, within the Charabanc structure specific roles were allowed to emerge 'within a context of necessity'[57] according to the inclinations and skills of the company member. Driven by common sense and their own brand of 'libertarian cultural activism'[58] they avoided many of the organisational difficulties and bitter dogmatic disputes which dogged the left-wing theatre movement in Britain during the 1970s.

Charabanc was always suspicious of the restrictions which might be imposed upon its work by prescriptive political labels such as 'Marxist' or 'feminist'. Indeed much has been made of the company's refusal to be described as a feminist theatre company. The truth is that, in 1983, they realised that such a designation would undoubtedly have alienated the conservative community audience which they sought to cultivate. Charabanc's motivation in recounting the story of the 1911 mill-girls' strike was, instinctively rather than overtly, socialist and pro-women rather than feminist. The play's subsequent success with working-class audiences justified the strategic necessity of this approach at that time.

However, not everyone appreciated Charabanc's efforts and ideology. Detractors immediately dismissed *Lay Up Your Ends* as 'agitprop' thereby displaying an incomplete understanding of the crude signification and abbreviated nature of that form. Gerry Colgan, reviewing the company's visit to the Dublin Theatre Festival for the *Irish Times* records a typical example of criticism levelled by an intellectual élite dismayed at the play's political intent and populist appeal:

> During the interval, a plummy voice from behind me assured its female companion that what we were watching was propagandist, might entertain the workers from Dunlop's, but was definitely, quite definitely, not art.[59]

The prevailing perception that what Charabanc was engaging with was 'not art' may, historically, account for the paucity of critical reflection devoted to the work of the company. However, the élitist attitudes of the 'plummy voices' responsible for canon-formation do not wholly explain why it has taken so long for Charabanc's plays to make it into print. Other examples of popular political theatre such as Martin Lynch's own *Dockers* have been published. It might be tempting to suggest that the female nature of the enterprise might have inhibited publication if it were not for the fact that Marie Jones' later solo work is widely available in print. However, if a perceived lack of serious cultural authority, for whatever reason, does not fully explain the long delay in publishing, it is fair to say that, until recently, the lack of Charabanc scripts in a printed, widely accessible form did not greatly assist those who had a genuine interest in writing about the company. In this the company may have shot itself in the foot by not publishing at an earlier stage for it is only through publication, academic scrutiny and the efforts of theatre historians that plays outlive the ephemeral nature of the theatrical experience. It is publish or be damned to oblivion.

 The reason for the long delay in getting this text from stage to page has its source in the politics of publishing and in Charabanc's origins as a theatre collective. Unlike its contemporary Field Day, Charabanc did not in 1983 have the time, resources or track-record as established writers to launch its first production into print. They were too busy getting the next show on the road on a shoestring budget to enter into negotiations with a publisher—had one been remotely interested at the time. Besides, 'joint efforts' were not perceived then to be as worthy of note as the single authorial voice. Publishers have traditionally been wary, sometimes with just cause, of the complex copyright wrangles posed by devised or collaborative play-scripts. As the years went on and the original company dispersed and moved successfully on with their individual careers, the concerted effort needed to get *Lay Up Your Ends* published seemed more and more unlikely to materialise. The play remained a fondly remembered, dog-eared manuscript on the shelves of the Theatre Archive of the Linenhall Library, Belfast—freely available, but only to those who knew where it was to be found. As the years went by, there was a very real danger that all trace of the play and its impact would eventually fade from memory. The advent of the twenty-fifth anniversary of the first performance of *Lay Up Your Ends* has provided the impetus to rescue the play from this fate.

It is now the hope of the founding-members of Charabanc that this publication will join Claudia Harris's anthology in encouraging productions of Charabanc's first and subsequent works. They also look forward to the play's inclusion on the curricula of schools and universities and to more widespread scholarly evaluation of the text. However, the decision to publish was not solely driven by a desire to provide an academic 'aide-memoire' or to preserve the text as a cultural document—important as those tasks may be. A play is only ever completely realised in production. It is the conviction of all those involved in this publication that revivals of *Lay Up Your Ends* will still have much to say to a twenty-first century audience.

Today's victims of appalling working conditions and exploitative employment practices are not the non-unionised female protagonists of *Lay Up Your Ends*, toiling for a pittance as they ingest the lung-rotting by-products of the wet-spinning process. Today's equivalents of these women are surely Ireland's migrant workers who pick mushrooms for a pound an hour whilst the bulk of their wages is creamed off by corrupt employment agencies in so-called 'accommodation costs'. They are the trafficked sex-workers held captive in a brothel in our own town. They are the Eastern European migrants on the streets of Belfast whose begging activities have been shown to be controlled by mafia-style godfathers. Everywhere it is evident that the powerful continue to exploit the weak and vulnerable for financial gain. In the 1980s it was the outrage at the inequities endured by female textile workers which fuelled the determination of Charabanc to document their story theatrically. It doesn't take a huge leap of the imagination to apply the experience of these women of a supposedly less enlightened age to that of more recent victims of greed and exploitation, thus making this play ripe for revival and re-interpretation.

Brenda Winter

Notes

[1]Harris, Claudia. *The Charabanc Theatre Company: Four Plays*. (Great Britain: Colin Smythe Ltd 2006)

[2]Byrne, Ophelia. *The Stage in Ulster from the Eighteenth Century* (Belfast: The Linenhall Library 1997) p.73

[3]Charabanc Collection, Linenhall Library, Belfast. Cat no. Char/SB/1

[4]Lojek, Helen. 'Playing Politics with Charabanc Theatre Company' in (eds.) Harrington, John P. and Mitchell, Elizabeth J. *Politics and Performance in Contemporary Northern Ireland* (Amhurst: University of Massachusetts 1999) p.91

[5]Byrne, Ophelia. *The Stage in Ulster* p.70

[6]Stalleybrass, Peter and White, Allon. *The Politics and Poetics of Transgression* (Ithaca: Cornell University Press 1986) p.5

[7]Ferriter, Diarmaid. *The Transformation of Ireland 1900-2000* (London: Profile Books 2004) p.722

[8]Urquhart, Diane. 'The Female of the Species is More Deadlier than the Male' in (eds.) Hayes, Alan and Urquhart, Diane. *The Irish Women's History Reader* (London and New York: Routledge 2001) p.51

[9]Interview with Marie Jones and Ian McElhinney, 22 June 2006. Tape in possession of writer.

[10]Cork Enquiry into Professional Theatre in England 1986.

[11]Foley, Imelda. *The Girls in the Big Picture* (Belfast: Blackstaff Press 2003) p.23

[12]Playzone was founded in 1977 by theatre director Andy Hinds, a graduate of Queen's University Belfast, and Dubliner Frank Brennan

[13]Kershaw, Baz. *The Politics of Performance: Radical Theatre as Cultural Intervention* (London: Routledge 1992) p.17

[14]Fitzgerald, Charles. *Belfast News Letter* 16 May 1983

[15]Connolly, Roy. *The Evolution of the Lyric Theatre Belfast* (Lampeter: The Edwin Mellen Press 2000) Appendix 2 p.250

[16]Byrne, Ophelia. *The Stage in Ulster* p.55

[17]Byrne, Ophelia. *The Stage in Ulster* pp. 55-63

[18]Arts Council Annual Report 1977-78 Public Records Office Northern Ireland

[19]Interview with Imelda Foley. Tape in the possession of the writer.

[20]McGrath John. *The Bone Won't Break : On Theatre and Hope in Hard Times* (London: Methuen 1990) p.142

[21]Kershaw, Baz. *The Politics of Performance* p.142

[22]Kershaw, Baz. *The Politics of Performance* pp. 59-60

[23]Kershaw, Baz. *The Politics of Performance* p.17

[24]Ibid.

[25]Grant, David. *Playing The Wild Card: A survey of community drama and smaller-scale theatre from a community relations perspective* (Northern Ireland Community Relations Council 1993) p.7

[26]Kershaw, Baz. *The Politics of Performance* p.5

[27]Connolly, Roy. *Lyric Players* p.205

[28]McGrath, John. *The Bone Won't Break* p.142

[29]McCready, Sam. In conversation with the writer.

[30]Lynch, Martin. *Dockers & Welcome to Bladonmore Road* (Belfast: Lagan Press 2003)

[31]Connolly, Roy. *Lyric Players* pp. 206-208

[32]Interview with Marie Jones and Ian McElhinney. 22 June 2006. Tape in the possession of the writer.

[33]The only record of this venture is a letter from the actress Sheila Hancock declining an invitation to become a patron of the Belfast Actors' Centre. Brenda Winter's personal papers.

[34]Eleanor Methven was away during this period working with Edinburgh Theatre Workshop.

[35]Morash, Christopher. *A History of Irish Theatre: 1601-2000.* (Cambridge: Cambridge University Press 2002) p.263

[36]Lynch, Martin. First Night Programme *Lay Up Your Ends*, Linenhall Library Belfast Cat. No. T/Charabanc 1. *Lay Up Your Ends* 1. Production File.

[37]Messenger, Betty. *Picking Up the Linen Threads* (Belfast: The Blackstaff Press 1988)

[38]Hepple, Peter. *The Stage* November 1984

[39]Heddon, Deirdre and Milling, Jane. *Devising Performance: A Critical History* (Basingstoke: Palgrave Macmillan 2006) p.18

[40]Brighton, Pam. 'Six Characters in Search of a Story' *Theatre Ireland* No. 6 (1984)

[41]*Irish Times*, 29 December 1987.

[42]*Irish Times*, 29 December 1987.

[43]'Lynch on Thursdays' *Irish News* (Charabanc Scrapbook Linenhall Library Belfast Cat. No. Char/SB/1)

[44]Fitzgerald, Charles. 'Impressive Women' *Belfast News Letter* 16 May 1983.

[45]First Night Programme *Lay Up Your Ends*, Charabanc Collection, Linenhall Library Belfast. Cat. No. T/Charabanc 1. *Lay up Your Ends* 1. Production File.

[46]Devlin, Paddy. *Irish News* 2 January 1984. Cutting in the possession of the writer.

[47]Turner, Victor. *From Ritual to Theatre: The Human Seriousness of Play* (New York: Performing Arts Journal 1982) pp. 44-48

[48]Carne, Rosalind. 'The Past Put Through the Mill' Stage Guardian 8 July 1983

[49]Interview with Marie Jones and Ian McElhinney, 22 June 2006. Tape in possession of writer.

[50]Wandor, Michelene. 'Cross-dressing, Sexual Representation...' in (ed) Goodman, *The Routledge Reader in Gender and Performance* (Oxford. Routledge 1998) p.171

[51]Fitzgerald, Charles The *Belfast News Letter* 16 May 1983

[52]Lojek, Helen. 'Playing Politics' in (eds) Harrington, John P. and Mitchell, Elizabeth J. *Politics and Performance* p.90

[53]*Ulad*. Editorial Vol.1 Nov. 1904

[54]Kershaw, Baz. *The Politics of Performance* p.139

[55]Heddon, Deirdre and Milling, Jane. *Devising Performance* p.52

[56]McGrath, John. 'Better a Bad Night in Bootle' *Theatre Quarterly* Vol. No. 15 (1975) pp.39-54

[57]Heddon, Deirdre and Milling, Jane. *Devising Performance: a Critical History* p.96

[58]Kershaw, Baz. *The Politics of Performance* p.150

[59]Colgan, Gerry, '*Lay Up Your Ends* at the John Player' Irish Times 7 October 1983

ERRATUM: [Footnote #34, Page 38]

The Publishers wish to make it clear that Eleanor Methven was in fact in Northern Ireland at this time. She did not go to Edinburgh until mid-February.

LAY UP YOUR ENDS
(1983)

Lay Up Your Ends was first performed by Charabanc Theatre Company at the Belfast Civic Arts Theatre on 15th May 1983. The play was directed by Pam Brighton. The music was by Dai Jenkins. The cast was as follows:

Florrie Brown	Eleanor Methven
Leadpipe	Dai Jenkins
Lizzie McCormick	Brenda Winter
Ethna McNamara	Carol Scanlan[†]
Mary Rooney	Maureen Macauley
Belle Thompson	Sarah Jones[†]

All other characters are played by the Company*

Time: Belfast, Ireland 1911

* The writers specify that subsidiary characters are played by women. In this text the name of the main character who played each subsidiary role in the original production is indicated in brackets at the point where that character first speaks. Where no name appears, then the role is taken by the actor playing Leadpipe.

[†] The actors Sarah Jones and Carol Scanlan now work professionally under the names Marie Jones and Carol Moore respectively. The latter names are used elsewhere in this edition.

ACT I

Scene 1

*The setting throughout is minimal (e.g. six wooden beer crates).
Hats, caps or shawls are used to effect character changes. For mill
scenes the women wear a mill-worker's apron with the tools of
their trade slung from the waist. Dim lighting. Five women enter
singing a mill song.*

Belfast mill, early,
Tramped the cold morning streets,
Thru' the mill gates, yawnin',
Same old walls to meet,
Fill up your trough, stand to your frame,
Grey Belfast mill.

Who'd be a Belfast spinner?
Feet in the water all day,

Tie up your bands,
Hawk up your yarn,
Pick out the laps,
Wet Belfast mill.

Look out for the spinning master,
Houl your carry on,
Whisht to your songs and chatter,
When Jim Doran's around,
Mind your frame, look to your yarn,
Lay up your ends,
Grey Belfast mill.

[*As the song fades and is held, there is the sound of a factory horn. Then the sound of the knocker-up is heard; we hear various responses from the women.*]

FLORRIE: Aye, all right, all right.

LIZZIE: Aye, I'm up.

MARY: I'm comin'; I'm comin'.

BELLE: Keep your hair on.

ETHNA: Is it that time?

[*Each woman exits after response. Immediately the sound of machinery is heard. The women enter (barefoot) and mime the spinning process. Presently a young boy enters carrying a brush and box and begins brushing the floor. Some of the women begin to use coarse sign language to each other in obvious reference to the boy. One woman fetches a tin of grease. Suddenly the women make a grab for the boy. After much squealing, laughing and struggling, the boy breaks loose and runs off. The women return to their machines laughing. The doffing mistress checks the machines.*]

MARY [*shouting over to* FLORRIE]: Florrie! Florrie! Have you any snuff?

[MARY *mimes sniffing snuff.* FLORRIE *nods and beckons her over.* MARY *takes a pinch.*]

BELLE: Mary Rooney! You better watch Jim Doran doesn't catch you on at that!

ETHNA: Hey Belle! This trough's stinkin'; you'd think somebody'd crawled into it and died!

BELLE: I saw Jim Doran washin' his trunks in it the other day!

MARY: Hey Belle, there's something stuck!

BELLE: Ethna! That'll be them! [BELLE *blows the whistle. Machine noise ceases.*] Thank Jasus, it's breakfast time!

ETHNA: Hey Mary, I was late out this morning. Y'wudn't gimme a drap o'your tea?

MARY [*ignoring her*]: Jesus, Ethna, you're always lukin' something.

FLORRIE: T'is great to get them machines aff all the same.

LIZZIE: You're just not used to workin' in the mill yet, Florrie Brown, that's what's wrong with you.

MARY: Country ones are always a bit slow to adapt. [*She notices* ETHNA *gazing longingly at her tea.*] Christsake, Ethna! [*She gives* ETHNA *the can.*]

BELLE: Here, I mind the time when I was younger, my da's people were from the country—out by Carrickfergus—and he used to take us down nigh and again. Well here dear, didn't this oul' farmer take a notion of me. He used til say to me ... [*She laughs at the memory.*]

FLORRIE: What?

BELLE: He used to say ... Isabelle—called me by m'full name an' all—Isabelle, you are like the lilies of the field.
[*The others laugh.*]

BELLE: Well, wait'll y'hear ... didn't he ask me to marry him, but I refused him.

MARY: And what happened?

BELLE: Didn't the oul' ghett buy himself a horse plough instead!
[*All laugh.* ETHNA *shrieks.*]

LIZZIE: Ethna! Will you for dear sake do somethin' about that laugh, my head's openin'.
[*The young boy returns and runs to grab the brush and box he left behind. Upon turning, he finds his way blocked by* BELLE, ETHNA *and* MARY. *As he breaks through,* MARY *chases him off stage.*]

BELLE: Mary Rooney! Will you catch yourself on!

MARY: Ach, it's only a bit of fun, Belle.

BELLE: It'll be some fun if Robbie Baker catches ye!

MARY: Ah, give over.

ETHNA: She'd shite herself if Robbie caught her lukin' at another man.

LIZZIE: And themins only a week away from the altar!

FLORRIE: Oh dear!

ETHNA: Stick-bracker, is he Mary?

LIZZIE: No, he is not. Robbie Baker's got a very good job; sure doesn't he drive for Cantrell and Cochrane?

FLORRIE: Did he take you to the Empire last night, Mary?

MARY: Aye, it was great.

ETHNA: Did you see the McDonald sisters?

MARY: Aye, they were brilliant. At the end y'know, that young fella Tom Allen—he goes up into the balcony and he sings down to Marie McDonald of the McDonald sisters.

FLORRIE: Way up in the balcony?

ETHNA: Aye, that's what he does; he goes up into the gods and sings down til her.

MARY: And she sings up to him. [*She sings the first few lines of* 'The Boy I Love is Up in the Gallery'.]

BELLE: Where's that wee fella for Mary, til she gets takin' his trousers off ... ?

LIZZIE: Ach, Belle, leave him alone.

FLORRIE: Ah Lizzie, it's only a bit of crack.

LIZZIE: Oh listen t'her, you'd think she was enjoyin' it or somethin'.

FLORRIE: Now, I'm only sayin' there's no real harm in it ...

BELLE: Course she's enjoyin' it!

MARY: We'll have to get her a man!

BELLE: Aye, Pinky Hewitt, the gate-man!

FLORRIE: Oh aye, yis are gettin' a quare rise outta me, aren't yis?

BELLE: Here Florrie, wud ye not like a big Belfast fella?

FLORRIE: You're a quare geg, Belle Thompson. I'll tell your man the carry on a ye!

MARY [*starting to sing.* BELLE *and* ETHNA *join in.*]

There was an ould woman, she lies alone

She lies alone

She lies alone.

There was an ould woman, she lies alone,

She wants a man but she can't get none.

FLORRIE [*pointing at* MARY]:

And now she's married and tied til a beg

And tied til a beg

And tied til a beg ...

[ETHNA *and* BELLE *grab* MARY. FLORRIE *gets some coarse yarn.*]

ETHNA: Hey Belle, get the bobbin'.

FLORRIE: Belle! Jim Doran's callin' you!

ETHNA: Frig it! We're on our break!

BELLE: Och, I'd better go and see what he wants.

[*She exits.* FLORRIE *and* LIZZIE *push raw flax down* MARY's *blouse while* ETHNA *holds her.*]

ETHNA: Hey Mary, has he got big feet?

LIZZIE: Aw now, Mary, y'know what they say about havin' big feet!

MARY: No?

LIZZIE: Well, you'll soon find out!

FLORRIE: Is he takin' you on the Bangor boat for your honeymoon, Mary?

ETHNA: Well, he'll not give her time to get sick anyway!

MARY: Ethna!

BELLE [*entering with a list of rules in her hand*]: Mary Rooney! Jim Doran wants to see you in his office.

[MARY *exits, taking the flax from her blouse.*]

LIZZIE: What's this, Belle?

BELLE [*handing* LIZZIE *the list of rules*]: Jim Doran says Mr Bingham sent them down. We've all to read them.

ETHNA: What does it say, Belle; what does it say?

LIZZIE [*reading*]: 'Any person found away from their usual place of work, except for necessary purposes, or talkin' with anyone out of their own alley will be fined 2d for each offence.' No singin'. You're not even allowed to stop to fix your hair.

[FLORRIE *takes list.*]

ETHNA: What? What are they on about? What does it say, Belle?

LIZZIE: It must be the new rules of the firm.

FLORRIE [*reading*]: 'All persons in our employ shall serve four weeks' notice before leavin' our employ, but E. Bingham and Company shall, and will, dismiss any person without notice being given.'

ETHNA: Does it say anythin' about breathin'? Are we still allowed to breathe?

FLORRIE: Aye, it's wild altogether.

ETHNA [*taking the list and giving it to* BELLE]: What about the fines, does it say any more about the fines?

BELLE [*reading*]: 'For every oath or insolent language—3d for the first offence and if repeated, they shall be dismissed.'

ETHNA: Frig's sake!

BELLE: Oh Jasus! Wait'll you hear this one Ethna! [*She pretends to read.*] 'All Catholics in the firm's employment over the age of thirty-five and with more than two children'—that's you—'will be obliged to leave the firm by the end of the week or join the Orange Order!'

ETHNA [*snatching rules*]: What? Oh my God! That's not fair— join the Orange Order? I've got eight childer, Belle!

BELLE: I'm only geggin'! [MARY *re-enters. She goes to* BELLE, *crying.*] What's wrong, love?

LIZZIE: What's happened, Mary?

MARY: I've been suspended!

BELLE: What?

LIZZIE: What for?

MARY: For carry on, he says.

LIZZIE: Och, sure it was all of us. He's always pickin' on that wee girl, whatever's wrong with him?

ETHNA: Any fines? Did he fine you anything? [MARY *shakes her head.*] Always fines me, every opportunity.

MARY: Ach, what am I goin' to do?

LIZZIE: Ach, she's savin' up.

FLORRIE: Aye, I know, it's awful.

LIZZIE: It's tarrible, the way they have you in here, tarrible.

BELLE: This is all Jim Doran's doin', whatever ails him. He's gone mad this last while back. Well, frig it! I've had enough of him!

LIZZIE: What can ye do; what can ye do?

BELLE: Stop work!

LIZZIE: What?!

BELLE: Well, why not? Isn't it about time this friggin' firm got a kick up the arse? B'Jasus I'm thirty-five years here—since I was eight years old—and niver once has them frames stopped, barrin' they were broke or gettin' cleaned!

LIZZIE: But Jim Doran'll go buck mad ... !

BELLE: Ah, I'm sick to the teeth of Jim Doran. I've been 'Yes, Jimmyin' 'n No, Jimmyin' all m'life; well b'Jasus it's gonna stop! And then there's this wee girl here—[*She indicates* MARY.]—well dar he—he'll soon change his tune when he sees them frames not gettin' switched on!

ETHNA: There's Jim Doran lukin' down on us nigh. [MARY *runs out.*] That'll be another fine. They'll be eatin' Fenton's tripe in our house for months nigh, wait'll you see!

[BELLE *goes to exit.*]

FLORRIE: Where are you going, Belle?

BELLE: Well, it's not up Jim Doran's arsehole, anyway!

[*Exit everyone except* FLORRIE *who moves into monologue spot.*]

FLORRIE: D'y'see thon Belle Thompson one? She'd start a row in an empty house, so she wud. Aye but like, forby that, she's one of the best all the same.

SUSIE (Ethna) [*offstage*]: Florrie!

FLORRIE: Susie dear, is it not about time you were tucked up?

SUSIE [*entering*]: I'm not one bit tired, Florrie!

FLORRIE: Now, it's past seven o'clock. I'll never get ye wakened for school the morra.

SUSIE: But I'm sick, Florrie. I don't want to go to thon oul' school.

FLORRIE: Here, let me feel your head. Aye you're a wee bit warm right enough. Wud a wee cuddle do the trick and put ye right? C'm'ere. [SUSIE *shrugs her off.*] Oh aye, you're all better now. Go an, run up them stairs before I shoot the boots off ye.

SUSIE: Florrie, are we stayin' here for ever and ever?

FLORRIE: Well, I don't know about for ever, Susie, but for a while.

SUSIE: Well, I don't like it, Florrie.

FLORRIE: Sure look at all the friends you have in the street. Isn't you and Peggy McNamara the great chums?

SUSIE: I don't like her; we're not on nigh.

FLORRIE: Oh aye? Here d'ye know what? Belle gave me a whole pile of oul' clothes for yousins.

SUSIE: Well I'm not wearin' them! I'm sick of oul' clothes. Why cud you not make me some pinnies? Our Mammy used to make me them.

FLORRIE: Aye well, Mammy's not here anymore.

SUSIE: Can we bring our Jack up here? You said when we came up here, you'd send for our Jack.

FLORRIE: Aye, I know Susie, but dogs don't like livin' in streets.

SUSIE: But you said ...

FLORRIE: Look, ye can't have Jack, now that's my last word on it. You're just bein' bold ...

SUSIE: But you said!

FLORRIE: Susie, that's enough! [SUSIE *exits in a huff.*] Aye well, Belfast's quare and different from home. At least on the farm you cud grow what y'cudn't buy. I never wanted to leave it, but like y'know yourselves, the eldest brother—that was our Walter—well, he'll always get the farm and then once he was married, there was no more use for me. So I took the wee brothers and sister, just like I promised Mammy I wud, and here we are in Belfast and thon mill. Aye well, if it wasn't here you wudn't ate and that's all about it. It's just being so closed in I can't stand. People's livin' one on top of the other in the wee streets—you never hardly see the sun. It's dark when you go in in the mornin' and dark when you're comin' out agin at nights. And there's this tightness with me in the house—four weeins all lukin' to me. Ah well, sure there's no use whinin' about it. Here, it's seven o'clock and not a weein washed.

She exits.

Scene 2

Barrel organ music and crowd noises set the scene at the Custom House steps. The five women enter, viewing the sights.

LIZZIE: Oh Belle, look, there's the herrin' seller. I must get some for Charlie's tea.

BELLE: C'mon Lizzie, there's them oul' Jehovah's Witnesses; they put the fear of God into me.

MARY: There's your man on his bed of nails.

ETHNA: Maybe it was him who punctured his arse last week.

BELLE [*addressing the audience*]: Sunday at the Customs House steps. The whole of Belfast was there; the place was black. There were tap-dancers on their wee boards, strong men, jugglers, 'Happy Jimmy' with his hurdy-gurdy—not forgettin' his monkey. And, of course, the street sellers bawlin' their brains out over the commotion ...

ETHNA: 'Herrin's, Ardglass herrin's, just 3d a pound. Fresh fish just in'—I love 'em.

MARY: 'Willicks, willicks, penny a bag, cooked and ready for eatin'—mmmmmmm.

[*She is about to tuck in when she notices* ETHNA *looking at her pleadingly and gives her one.*]

BELLE: And, of course, no Sunday would be complete without the Salvation Army. [*The three actresses play* 'Onward Christian Soldiers' *on imaginary instruments.* LIZZIE *sings.*] And the Holy Joes trying in vain to convert everyone.

PREACHER (Florrie): Leviticus, Chapter 12 and Verse 11—'He who uncovers his father's wife's brother, uncovers the nakedness of his father'.

BELLE: And the politicians spoutin' on as usual. [*Politican speaks enthusiastic and sincere gobbleygook.*] Aye, you get all

sorts down at the Custom House steps—most of them
lookin' money.

ETHNA: Hey Mary, what the hell's that?

[*A brightly coloured booth 'walks' onstage.*]

MARY: Here, there's writin' here.

ETHNA: What does it say, Mary; what does it say?

MARY: 'Put coin in slot'.

ETHNA: A coin? What for?

MARY: 'And be amazed'.

ETHNA: It's only one of them money grabbers, Mary. C'mon, the
man's going to put his arse on the bed of nails over there ...

MARY: Ach, wait for us, Ethna. I'm goin' to put a halfpenny in ...

LIZZIE: Mary, you're supposed to be savin' up t'get married!

ETHNA: Mary, you're mad! Mary!

[*As* MARY *inserts coin a flap comes down and a man's face appears
playing a few bars of a rowdy tune on a toy bugle. He closes the
flap abruptly.*]

ETHNA [*screaming with laughter*]: Do it again, Mary! Do it again!

MARY: I haven't got another halfpenny.

ETHNA: Belle, put another halfpenny in.

BELLE: Away and suck my big toe, Ethna!

[*The look on* LIZZIE's *face tells* ETHNA *she'd better not ask her.*]

ETHNA: Florrie, have you got one?

FLORRIE: Away on, Ethna, you're jokin'.

MAN [*appearing again at the flap*]: I wonder wud yous take
yerselves off outta this. I'm tryin' to run a business here.

BELLE: Here—we've a right to stand here like anybody else—
it's a free country.

MAN [*closes flap*]: You cheeky friggin' trollop! [*He comes round
the side of the booth.*] Go on now, clear off outta this; go on,
away and rattle! [*The women fold their arms and stand their
ground.*] Yis are a shower of dirty millies, so yis are—I'll take

my business elsewhere! [*He returns to the booth and 'walks' offstage while the women shout abuse.*]

FLORRIE: Business he calls it! I've seen better yokes than that at the Lammas Fair!

LIZZIE: Cheek!

BELLE: Go on, you can't even play yer oul' bugle!

MARY: Give us back me halfpenny, y'oul' robber!

ETHNA: I mind him when he'd no arse in his trousers!

BELLE [*to audience*]: Now on this particular Sunday ...

LIZZIE: Hey look, I wonder what's goin' on over there. Is it somebody speakin'?

FLORRIE: God knows.

BELLE: Shush! til we hear what he's saying! [*Starting to relay the speech*] 'The worker is the slave of the Capitalist Society—the female worker is the slave of that slave.'

ETHNA: It's only somebody talkin'.

MARY: Good lukin' big fella, isn't he?

BELLE: 'Where there is a big demand for female labour, the woman ends up doing two jobs.'

FLORRIE: Aye, he can say that again.

MARY: I like his moustache.

BELLE: 'Overworked, underpaid and badly nourished, she falls prey to all the diseases that infect the badly constructed hovels of the poor.'

ETHNA: He musta bin in our house!

LIZZIE: My house is not a hovel!

BELLE: 'Of what stuff are these Belfast women made—who refuse to unite together to do something about their conditions?'

LIZZIE: Who does he think he is? C'mon Florrie, I'm away!

FLORRIE: Aye. You right, Belle?

BELLE: Aye, I'll follow yis—'The great only remain great because we are on our knees.'

ETHNA: I'd love to know what that man was on about.

LIZZIE: He's talkin' through his hat!

FLORRIE: C'mon you.

[*They exit.*]

MARY: He is a good-lookin' fella but.

BELLE: Name a God! It's as well he doesn't hackle flax in York Street Mill. Mary Rooney wud have him harrished! D'ye see if Robbie Baker hasn't her lyin' wi' a child before the summer, it'll not be her fault! I'll see yis!

MARY: Belle!

ETHNA: Hey Mary, don't you be pickin' up some wee fella down the street, d'ye hear me!

MARY: I shud be so lucky.

[*She exits.*]

ETHNA: See ya in the morning. [ETHNA *turns and is confronted by the figure of* HUMPY HESSIE, *the moneylender.*] Jasus! Hessie McGowan, m'heart!

HESSIE (Belle): C'mon Ethna McNamara, you owe me two weeks nigh.

ETHNA: I'll tell ye what it is, Hessie, he'd a broken pay this week and I'd two fines aff me in the mill.

HESSIE: Where's m'money?

ETHNA: I'll pay you on Monday—I'm takin' in some washin' and I'll clear ye then, I swear to God I will.

HESSIE: I've been too soft w'you. I'm goin' round nigh to tell your man.

ETHNA: Hessie, wait! Just one more day?

HESSIE: Y'better!

They exit.

Scene 3

Loud mill machine noises are heard as women enter one by one and hang up their shawls. LIZZIE *enters last, looking ill.*

LIZZIE: Belle, I'm not feelin' well at all.

BELLE: Maybe you should go home, Lizzie.

LIZZIE: Some chance!

FLORRIE: That's what you get for havin' babies.

ETHNA: You shud do what I do, Lizzie; I've stopped!

BELLE: You've stopped?

ETHNA: Aye, I don't let him near me.

BELLE: I'd love to believe ye. I cud just picture big Alfie McNamara—[*In disbelief*] 'I don't let him near me'!!

ETHNA: I don't let him near me when he's sober.

FLORRIE: How do you work that one out?

ETHNA: A keep him drunk! [*The others laugh.*] What do you think has me in debt and danger with Hessie McGowan this last while back? Since my last one was born in May I made up my mind, no more childer. Eight's enough for any wee girl. But he wudn't hear tell of it.

BELLE: I thought it was the doctor told ye to stop.

ETHNA: Oh aye, he told me that too; he said a wasn't worth tuppence after the last one. He said ... know what he said? ... said I'd have to stop lyin' with Alfie. [*All laugh.*] So I went home and I said to him, 'I'm movin' in with the weeins.'

FLORRIE: And what happened?

ETHNA: Pig beat me black and blue!

MARY: Why didn't you brain him with something?

LIZZIE: That's one thing a can honestly say. In all the days I've been married t'him, Charlie McCormick has never laid a finger on me.

ETHNA: I get it that often, I was thinkin' I might as well go the whole hog and take up professional boxin'. Like I'm gettin' quare and good at jukin' and jumpin' outta the way. And a can take a punch. That's one thing, a can take a quare punch.

LIZZIE: I'm gonna be sick!

[LIZZIE *rushes off.* FLORRIE *moves to* LIZZIE'*s frame.*]

FLORRIE: That's a tarrible way to have to carry on w'your own man.

ETHNA: At least I've bloody well got one!

BELLE: Tell thesins, and I'll go up and tell the reelers.

ETHNA: Tell us what?

[BELLE *exits.*]

FLORRIE: Belle heard a rumour last week that all the mills is goin' on shorter hours. And the two of us was told today that it's nearly certain from next week onwards that they're gonna take eight and a quarter hours a week off us!

ETHNA: Ah frig!

MARY: Eight and a quarter hours?

FLORRIE: That's a loss of over two shillin's a week!

ETHNA: Two shillin's! How am I supposed t'manage on that?

MARY: That's my weddin' money up in the air.

FLORRIE: Well, I've worked out that I'm gonna have til buy more tripe and bacon, for sausages is out.

ETHNA: Sausages out, Florrie? Food's out!

FLORRIE: Instead of gettin' the odd Barney Hughes loaf, I'm gonna have til bake everything m'self and where am a gonna get all the time?

ETHNA: Two shillin's outta m'money! I'll have til give the childer up til the poor house. Let them keep them.

FLORRIE: We'll all be joinin' ye, Ethna.

MARY: Flip, waita Robbie hears this!

ETHNA: I'm not payin' m'rent!

FLORRIE: You can't do that, Ethna.

ETHNA: Why not? It's themins what owns the houses and it's themins what are takin' the two shillin's out of our money. They can't crucify us altogether.

FLORRIE: Well, it's supposed to be that the women in Blackstaff and Jennymount's and all is all ragin' about it! [LIZZIE *enters.*] Are ye all right? Did ye get it up?

MARY: How are ye?

ETHNA: Have y'heard, Lizzie? They're takin' two shillin's aff us ...

LIZZIE: Flip sake, I'm all right! As long as Jim Doran doesn't see me not able for m'work. [*She goes back to her frame and starts working.*]

FLORRIE: Accordin' to Mary Galway, the mill's trade's been fallin' off. They say there's too much pilin' up in the warehouse and they have to cut back on production.

BELLE [*entering, in time to hear what* FLORRIE *is saying*]: That's what you shud tell your Alfie, Ethna, next time he's lukin' his way w'ye—'Hey Alfie, the house's full up, I'm cuttin' production!' [*All laugh.*] Mary Rooney, Jim Doran wants to see you in his office.

[MARY *exits.*]

FLORRIE: What's this next?

BELLE: God knows. Probably wants to fine her for something or other.

FLORRIE: He has that wee girl tortured. Never leaves her alone, whatever he has agin her.

[MARY *re-enters.*]

BELLE: Well?

MARY: I have t'go. Said my suspension's not up. I shudn't have come into work.

BELLE: Bastard!

FLORRIE: He said two days!

MARY: Says nigh it's until he sends for me.

[MARY *exits.*]

LIZZIE: In the name a God.

BELLE: He can't do that!

LIZZIE: He's done it.

ETHNA: I'd love to shove this picker up his arse!

FLORRIE: Poor Mary. Is there nothin' we can do to help her? It's not fair; it isn't right.

[*Silence*]

BELLE: Right girls, frig it; get your shawls! [*Silence*] I said, get your shawls!

ETHNA: It's only six o'clock, Belle.

BELLE [*lifting the shawls*]: Shut up, Ethna. Come on Lizzie, you too.

LIZZIE: Belle, for God's sake!

ETHNA: You're only jokin', Belle, aren't ye?

FLORRIE [*brightening up*]: No Ethna, she's not jokin'! [*She puts on her shawl.*]

ETHNA: Jesus, Mary and Joseph, are we walkin' out, Belle? Sware til God, you're not geggin'!

BELLE: Run quick and catch Mary. Oul' itchy balls is not gettin' away with this.

[ETHNA, BELLE *and* FLORRIE *exit.* LIZZIE *is left alone. She waits for a minute, then hurriedly lifts her shawl and runs off.*]

Scene 4

Scene change as the women enter LIZZIE's *house.*

BELLE: Here he'll be. [*She starts to mimic* JIM DORAN.] Mr
Bingham ... [*Scratches her backside*] ... Mr Bingham, it wasn't
my fault. They just walked out. [*She picks her nose.*] Will a
sack them, will a sack them?

[*All the women laugh, except* LIZZIE.]

FLORRIE: Be a laugh if it was him that got sacked!

[*More laughter*]

ETHNA: Sure as God, I thought I was gonna die laughin'!

MARY: I think I've wet myself!

[*More laughter*]

BELLE: The walk-out spread like wildfire, didn't it?

MARY: Didn't half.

FLORRIE: And they've come out up at Jennymount too.

BELLE: A friggin' strike in York Street Mill; I niver thought I'd
see the day! It was friggin' great, wasn't it? [*Pause*] Right,
first things first; Lizzie, make a wee cup of tea.

LIZZIE: I'm not makin' tea, get away. I don't know how you
can think of tea at a time like this. The polis'll be in on us
any minute.

FLORRIE: Lizzie sit down for God's sake or you'll have the rest
of us like yourself.

[LIZZIE *can't settle. She paces the floor behind them.*]

ETHNA: What are we gonna do, Belle? Will they fine us? Do you
think they'll fine us?

LIZZIE: Fine us? Ethna McNamara! That's the first time I mind
that anybody's ever walked out of that mill and you're
talkin' about fines! As sure as hell, I think they'll hang a
couple of us!

ETHNA: How are we gonna get the money to pay for the fines? It'll be hundreds taking us all together; it'll be hundreds a pounds.

MARY: And I'd like to know what we're gonna live on if this strike lasts any length a time? I've a wedding to pay for on Saturday.

LIZZIE: A good question. Even if they did let us go on strike, what are we gonna live on? You can't eat fresh air!

ETHNA: Mine's tried it! They have, Belle, many's a time they've had it til do.

LIZZIE: And what'll happen our houses? The mill owns the houses we live in, remember?

FLORRIE: Hold on, hold on. One thing at a time, Lizzie.

MARY: What if they sack the lot of us? Like there are hundreds of weemin who wud give their right arms for our jobs.

LIZZIE: Why don't yis get in touch with Mary Galway and her society?

BELLE: What for?

LIZZIE: To speak to Mr Bingham for us, that's what for.

BELLE: You've a hope in hell—Miss Mary Galway of the Society of Textile Operatives is about as useful as a wooden poker! All she does is organise wee clubs for the girls, make sure the workers have no nits in their hair. She doesn't want to have no truck with the bosses, that's why she steers clear of the spinners, reelers, rovers and doffers—the ordinary mill-girls.

FLORRIE: So we're out on our own then?

BELLE: Aye, like a bunch of lepers.

FLORRIE: Then we'll have to sort somethin' out among ourselves.

LIZZIE: Could we not ask Miss Galway to spake for us?

MARY: Aye, there'd be no harm in askin'.

FLORRIE: Aye, I think we shud.

ETHNA: Y'have to get somebody to spake for ye, like ye can't go on strack and everything and not have somebody to spake for ye. Like, the moneylenders wudn't like it neither if there was nobody to pay them. Everything wud go to wreck an' ruin if the moneylenders weren't paid, wudn't it, Belle?

BELLE: How 'bout that fella at the Custom House steps? Now he was talkin' about the mills' conditions, wasn't he?

FLORRIE: They call him Connolly.

BELLE: What about going to see him and see if he'll put his money where his mouth is?

LIZZIE: In the name of God, as if we're not bad enough and you're talkin' about bringin' in strangers! He's from the South, y'know. Mr Bingham wudn't be one bit pleased.

ETHNA: That's the God's truth. Mr Bingham wud be tarrible annoyed.

FLORRIE: Well look, all right we cud talk all day about who'd like it and who wudn't, but it doesn't really halp us much this minute. Cud some of us not go and see Miss Galway and Mr Connolly and see what both have to say?

ETHNA: Why don't you do it, Florrie, you and Belle; yis have the cheek.

MARY: Aye, Florrie and Belle.

FLORRIE [*to* BELLE]: Cud we do that?

BELLE: Aye, don't see why not. It's the squeakin' wheel that gets the oil.

FLORRIE: What are we gonna say?

ETHNA: Aye, what are we gonna say? Like I'm sittin' here and I'm not even sure what we're strackin' over, know what I mane? Mary, know what a mane? If I was to go home to him, I cudn't even tell him what the strack's over.

FLORRIE: So what's the main thing we're askin' for?

BELLE: Well, I wudn't mind two weeks' paid holiday a year.

[*They all laugh.*]

MARY: I think if they're gonna cut our hours, they shud cut them all on one day and maybe we'd get that day off.

FLORRIE: Aye, they cud give us Saturdays off altogether instead of takin' a few hours off every mornin' and still bringin' us in six days a week.

MARY: Aye, Saturdays off.

FLORRIE: So we all want Saturdays off?

[*All nod and say* 'Aye'.]

LIZZIE: I don't agree. Yis'll never get it; I don't care what yis say.

ETHNA: What about all that carry on about not bein' allowed to talk in work or stop to fix yer hair or anythin'?

BELLE: And not bein' allowed to go to the toilet without permission. We shud all make our water at the one time in the middle of the floor and rub oul' hairy nose's bake in it.

[*All laugh.*]

MARY: And what harm is there in a bit of singin'?

FLORRIE: We want all them rules threw out, then?

[*All nod and say* 'Aye'.]

LIZZIE: Nigh, yis know that's goin' too far.

BELLE: And we're definitely not goin' back without Mary!

[*All agree with* 'Aye's.]

FLORRIE: At least now we know where we are. We've a list of things to tell them we're not one bit happy with.

ETHNA: But what are we gonna do the marra? Like, I'm sure there'll be ones goin' in to work who don't even know about the strack.

MARY: That's right.

FLORRIE: Well, when are we gonna put our things to Mr Bingham?

BELLE: First thing in the mornin', why not?

LIZZIE: He'll not meet yis.

BELLE: That's his luk out.

FLORRIE: Y'know if we see Mr Bingham and he decided he was goin' to be decent about it, it wud just be a matter of goin' in to work as usual.

MARY: Oh aye, that's different.

ETHNA: You niver know, there mighten be any cause til strack at all, Belle; mighten be any need for it, Mary.

BELLE: If Mr Bingham agrees to all our things, I'll lick Jim Doran's arse every dinner hour til I retire.

LIZZIE: C'mon Florrie, hurry it up; he'll be through this door any minute.

FLORRIE: Right, so we all turn up for work in the mornin' as usual and if Mr Bingham doesn't listen to our points, we stay out?

[*All agree.*]

BELLE: We'll march up and down outside.

MARY: We'll get writin' done and all and hold them up to let everybody know what we want.

FLORRIE: And maybe a big meetin' to let all the girls hear everything.

[*They all agree.* BELLE *winks.*]

BELLE: And here, I forgot, another wee thing shud be added on. I think we shud put somethin' in about the moneylenders.

ETHNA [*excited*]: Debts, aye debts, Belle.

BELLE: Like, there's some of us is in tarrible debt. How much do you owe, Ethna?

ETHNA: Oh ... am ... I don't know ... it's a quare lot, like.

BELLE: Well, I think we shud stay out til Mr Bingham clears up every penny and lifts all our things outta the pawn.

ETHNA: Yes, aye, aye Belle, the pawn too, that'd be a quare oul' mark. Wha'da you think Florrie? Is Belle right in what she's sayin'?

[FLORRIE *cannot keep her face straight. They all burst out laughing.*]

FLORRIE: She's havin' ye on, Ethna.

ETHNA: I knew; I knew. See that Belle Thompson one, I know not to listen to her.

LIZZIE: Is that it nigh, Florrie? He's gonna walk in on us.

FLORRIE: That's it, Lizzie. So we all come together tomorrow mornin' outside the mill?

[*All agree and stand.*]

BELLE: I can't wait to see oul' hairy nose's face when he sees a thousand angry women in the middle of York Street.

ETHNA: I'll call for you, Lizzie.

LIZZIE: I think you've all gone mad.

Scene 5

All the women except LIZZIE *enter carrying placards and singing.*

> Oul' Bingham thought he had us with his rules and cuts,
> Oul' Bingham thought he had us with his rules and cuts,
> Oul' Bingham thought he had us, but you see
> > he didn't get us
> With his rules, rules, rules and cuts.

BELLE [*jumping on a box to speak to the crowd*]: Right girls, as far as I'm concerned we're well and truly out on strike. [*The women cheer.*] Bingham has as much as declared war agin us with his shorter hours and fines and suspensions and rules and demands and one thing and another. Well, if it's a fight he wants, it's a fight he's gonna get! [*The women cheer.*] Nigh, there's a few things yis all shud know, so I'm gonna ask Florrie Brown to have a few words with yis.

[*While* BELLE *and* FLORRIE *speak to each other the crowd sings again.* BELLE *calms them down.*]

FLORRIE: I just want to report that Belle Thompson and me has been to see Mary Galway of the Textiles Union and James Connolly of the Workers' Union and here's what both of them has to say. Mary Galway wants us to go back to work so's that she can start talkin' to Mr Bingham about our points. But, she says we'll not get nowhere if we stay out on strack.

BELLE: She's talkin' through her arse!

ETHNA: Sure, I thought we weren't goin' back to work.

FLORRIE: Now, Mr Connolly, he says we have every right to strack and if we were to form ourselves into a union, he'd give us every help he cud and he says we're bound to win if we stick together. [*The women cheer.*] He says the first thing we have to do is to start up a strack fund.

ETHNA: I seconds that.

FLORRIE: Mr Connolly says we're goin' to need a strack fund to see us through the worst days of the strack. We have to start collectin' in every part of this city. At the shipyards, the docks, the engineerin' firms and even dure to dure as well.

BELLE: And we're startin' our own wee strike band wi' members from different bands ... if you know what I mean? [*Voices in crowd agree.*]

FLORRIE: It all adds up to us startin' our own union.

MARY: We'll start our own union.

ETHNA: Up Connolly!

FLORRIE: I think we'd all have to be bloody stupid not to go along with James Connolly of the Workers' Union.

[*The women cheer.* FLORRIE *steps down and* BELLE *takes over.*]

BELLE: Girls, we've made up all our points and I say we stick til them til the bitter end! [*The women cheer.*] We've all got wee families and God knows half of them is runnin' about half-lost and half-starved as it is. The wans what owns them mills has made a great fortune outta sellin' their fancy linen all over the world. Isn't it us what makes that linen? Isn't it only right that we get a fair slice of the cake? [*The women cheer and shout 'hear, hear'.*] And if Bingham wants to lock them gates, let him! Cause we're out on strack, the whole two thousand of us and we're stayin' out!

[*The women cheer. As* BELLE *steps down they sing.*]

Cheer up, Belle,
No matter what you do,
Don't let Bingham
Throw it on to you,
For if you do, you will rue,
So cheer up, Belle,
No matter what you do.

[LIZZIE *is seen approaching. She looks embarrassed.*]

LIZZIE [*speaking to the audience*]: They did it. I dunno what Charlie's mother's gonna say—and my mother too, God rest her. She always used to say, 'Get til your work and keep yourself to yourself'. Great woman, my mother. I idolised the ground she walked on. She always made sure I'd a nice clean shawl round me—ach, just like you'd do yersel', missus, wi' your own. It was her started me on the crochetin' just like I'm doin' wi' my Ginny nigh. Makes awful good bedspreads. Charlie's mother always used to say, 'Elizabeth, ye cud ate mate off thon toilet seat, it's that clean.' And so ye cud—for I'm all for the house—well, I've even got a wee bit of brass. D'ye know, I wudn't be afeard to bring King George in for a drap a tea. Course his Ma thought he was marryin' beneath him—what with the wee bit of extra schoolin' an all. But it cud niver be said that I kept a dirty house or that the children went hungry. She herself started as a half-timer in this very mill—the best damask weaver this side of the Lagan. I've a wee bit of hers in the house that I keep special like, in case we have a wee bit of a join. See Mr Bingham in there; I'm sure he has some lovely pieces about his house. Supposed to have a beautiful garden. Has a gardener to do his roses in the summer. Great family man. Three lovely childer. I'm sure he's awful proud. Course Belle wud say I'm only lickin' his arse, but fair's fair, we all have to live together in this world. And as my Charlie says, leave it to the ones that knows best. Still, once they take to cuttin' the hours, it's hard to know what to do for the best. Like, I wudn't like them thinkin' I'm all for myself.

[*The women begin singing.* LIZZIE *takes her placard. They all walk round and exit.*]

Fall in and follow me, fall in and follow me,
Never mind the weather, all together,
All together, stand by me boys,
I know the way to go
I'll take you for a spree,
You do as I do and you'll do right,
So fall in and follow me.

Scene 6

In the mill-owner's office. MR BINGHAM *and* JIM DORAN *are talking.*

BINGHAM (Lizzie): Are they determined?

DORAN (Ethna): Very, Mr Bingham.

BINGHAM: Who ... who's behind the whole thing?

DORAN: Well, as you know, they're all out nigh, every single one of them. That's one thousand seven hundred and twenty-five weemin. But if you're wantin' my opinion, personally like, I've no doubt it all started in the spinning room. Two weemin by the name of Belle Thompson and Florrie Brown. Florrie Brown's been here six months. A fine-lukin' big girl.

BINGHAM: I'm not interested in her physical attributes, Mr Doran.

DORAN: Beg your pardon, sir.

BINGHAM: And you think they're determined?

DORAN: I've niver seen them in the mood they're in nigh.

BINGHAM: If ... if it was up to you, Mr Doran, what would you do?

DORAN: Me, Mr Bingham?

BINGHAM: Yes, you.

DORAN: I'd ... give them the Saturdays off, Mr Bingham.

BINGHAM: I beg your pardon!

DORAN: They're in a terrible mood, Mr Bingham.

BINGHAM: And so am I!

DORAN: I don't blame ye, Mr Bingham, but I can't see us gettin' round it any other way.

BINGHAM: I can't give them Saturdays off. Probably wouldn't know what to do with it anyway. We have a principle of a six-day week and that must be maintained. By the way, how have they reacted to the new list of rules?

DORAN: That's what's worse, Mr Bingham. The shorter hours is nothin' to them not bein' allowed to talk and sing and what have ye.

BINGHAM: It's worked then?

DORAN: I don't think I know what you're talkin' about, Mr Bingham.

BINGHAM: I needed the hours shortened, didn't I?

DORAN: That's what you've said, what with the fallin' off in trade and that.

BINGHAM: And it was fairly obvious the workers would feel disconcerted, wasn't it?

DORAN: If you knew half the abuse I've taken, Mr Bingham.

BINGHAM: Well, that's why I did it!

DORAN: To make them more angry?

BINGHAM: No! To take their minds off the shortened hours and the cut in wages.

DORAN [*beginning to smile*]: I niver thought of that, Mr Bingham.

BINGHAM: I'm sure the girls like to comb their hair regularly?

DORAN: Half a' them niver stops. [*Laughs*]

BINGHAM: And even a dog needs to bark from time to time? [DORAN *continues to be amused by this.*] I like to sing occasionally myself. [DORAN *is still laughing.* BINGHAM *changes his mood instantly. Angrily*]: What are you laughing at, Doran?

DORAN: Sorry sir, sorry Mr Bingham.

BINGHAM: I think you can go now and meet our disconcerted workers.

DORAN: Right sir, goin' nigh. [*He goes to leave.*]

BINGHAM: Oh, Mr Doran. [DORAN *returns.*] Remember the names of the ring-leaders, would you?

DORAN [*pointing at his temple*]: Well remembered, Mr Bingham, well remembered. [BINGHAM *exits while* DORAN *moves downstage.* FLORRIE *and* BELLE *enter.*] The very two I wanna see.

BELLE: Well, we don't wanna see you.

FLORRIE: Where's Mr Bingham?

DORAN: You don't think that a man as busy as Mr Bingham is goin' to parley with the likes of you?

FLORRIE: He'll have to if he wants his machines to go.

BELLE: We've been asked by the girls til spake t'him.

DORAN: And I've been asked b'Mr Bingham to spake to you.

Look, he wants to make it clear, just in case anybody's still not sure of his intentions, that York Street Mill belongs to Mr Eric Bingham and Company Limited. And while it does, he will run the mill as and how he sees fit. He further points out that any employee who wants to leave the firm is free as and from here and nigh to do so.

BELLE: Who the hell ... ?

FLORRIE: Just a minute, we're entitled to ... !

DORAN: Girls, that's enough! Mr Bingham has no more to say at this point in time. As far as he's concerned the mill gates is closed and they only open when he decides. All right? [*He goes to exit past the women.*]

BELLE: You sicken the arse off me, Jim Doran!

[DORAN *stops and stares at* BELLE.]

FLORRIE: Well, you tell Mr Bingham from us, Mr Doran, that there's nearly two thousand women out there and each and every one of them is determined to see justice done here. We're formin' ourselves into a union and the next time we go through them gates it'll be after we've won this strike! C'mon Belle.

BELLE: Aye, and you'd better houl on til your trousers when we do come back.

[DORAN *exits singing.*]

FLORRIE: Well, it looks like we're out on strike now, whether we like it or not.

BELLE: Doesn't that give you some idea what Eric Bingham thinks of the mill-girls? C'mon Florrie, battle plans!

[*They enter* GINNY's *pub.*]

BELLE: Two porter, Ginny.

GINNY (Mary) [*offstage*]: Right y'be, Belle.

BELLE: Nigh, I can't stay long, Florrie; I've to go and wash Nora McClenaghan's man down, God rest his soul.

FLORRIE: God, Belle, is it you that washes down the dead bodies?

BELLE: Well somebody has to do it. Ye can't have them goin' to meet their maker piggin'!

FLORRIE: It wud give me the willies.

BELLE: Ach, you get used to it. It's just like scrubbin' your step.

FLORRIE: Here, what do yis do about ... men?

BELLE: Well, they can't do you no harm when they're dead. Though, I mind one oul' fella from Nile Street. Sufferin' Alec! They'd a brave job gettin' the lid of the coffin closed. They near had to put a wee hole in the lid of it. Ach, he always had a wee want in him anyway.

[GINNY *enters with the drink.*]

GINNY: Two bottles of porter.

FLORRIE: In the name a Jasus, Ginny, I thought you were brewin' that yourself!

GINNY: Well, what about this strike, then?

BELLE: Aw goin' great guns, Ginny—d'ye know we've got the whole of York Street Mill out nigh?

GINNY: Aye, I heard the commotion this morning passin' my door. Singin' and carryin' on—sounds like you were havin' a rare oul' time?

BELLE: Ach, sure you wudn't get as much fun down at the Empire. [*She begins to search for money.*]

GINNY: Not at all, daughter dear. Sixims never reared Ginny Murphy. I'm supportin' the strike.

FLORRIE: Good luck to ya, Ginny.

GINNY [*as she exits*]: Oh aye, I'm supporting the mill-girls all right!

BELLE: God love ya, Ginny, God love ya.

FLORRIE: Did you see themins in Royal Avenue this mornin'? They were stoppin' and cheerin' us on.

BELLE: Aye, an' the ones in the tramcar at Castle Junction, wavin' away at us they were.

FLORRIE: I hope it lasts.

BELLE: Wha'd'ya mean?

FLORRIE: I mean I hope the girls can stick it out. Luk, I can't see the likes of Eric Bingham cowin' down to a crowd of weemin overnight.

BELLE: He's goin' to have to, Florrie. There's two thousand weemin on the streets. You heard what Connolly said—it's the workers in any great city that makes it great. Like, who is it that builds the ships on the island, eh? Who is it what loads and unloads the ships and everything? Great industrial Belfast wud be nothin' without the workers. It makes ye think, like, it makes ye think. D'ye know somethin', Florrie? This has to stop somewhere or the bloody machines we're workin' will be gettin' more respect than us.

FLORRIE: Well, just look at us, Belle. It's us what makes the finest linen in the world but we can't afford to bring it home w'us.

BELLE: Linen? I've two sheets of brown paper on my windys and the *Telegraph* coverin' the table. [*She slugs at the bottle.*] C'mon Florrie, we've work to do. [FLORRIE *exits.* BELLE *moves into monologue spot.*] I'm goin' down nigh to wash down big Jim McClenaghan. He used to be the best-lookin' hackler that ever walked York Street til the pouce got him. Thirty-five years of age. Ah, he's happy done for. I've seen manys a one sufferin' on, coughin' their guts up, not bein' able to get a breath with th'oul flax. It's a tarrible death. I'll tell yis one thing, there's no chance of Bingham bein' laid up with the pouce or the mill fever. Thirty-five years I've worked in that mill and I've hardly ever clapped eyes on him. He lives in a big house up the Antrim Road. I seen it for myself goin' out on the tramcar to Glengormley—me eyes near drapped outta me head. Do you know, he has a garden you cud put a street of our wee houses in. Course, ye get wans like Lizzie who says, 'If it wasn't for Mr Bingham we wudn't have jobs'. Well I don't give a damn. No one man shud have all that money when the ones that made it for him haven't even got what wud put a meal's mate on the table. And him sittin' up there on his arse wi' all that money, probably big lumps of steak every night for his dinner and big Jim McClenaghan lyin' in a box through doin' his day's work. Well that's not fair. D'ye see if I was to say this to Bingham— he'd laugh at me. But by God he'd laugh on the other side of his face if every man, woman and child that works in them mills said, 'We're not goin' through them gates, not until we get what's due til us.' Well, then he'd listen, 'cause he'd have to, for he has a hell of a lot to lose.

Look at us, look around ye, what d'ye see? Prosperous Belfast, eh? Like, I'm not too good at the sums but I'll tell yis what I do know—ye can't take nothin' away from nothin'.

Scene 7

FLORRIE, LIZZIE, MARY *and* LEADPIPE (*playing a drum*) *come onstage rattling collection boxes and singing* 'Fall In and Follow Me'.

FLORRIE: C'mon, get your hands in yer pockets! A penny for the strikers! C'mon now!

BELLE: C'mon, a penny for the union! [*She notices* LIZZIE *hesitating behind.*] C'mon Lizzie!

LIZZIE: I never thought I'd see the day I'd be out on the streets beggin'.

BELLE: Ach, Lizzie, I haven't had as much fun since Ernie McCrum's wake!

MARY: Support the York Street Mill girls!

LORRIE: We're gettin' quare support.

LIZZIE [*weakly*]: Support the strike! Support the strike! C'mon!

MARY: And to think that oul' doll, Mary Galway, said we shudn't be street collectin'.

BELLE: If we listened to her, we'd be goin' back in with less than we came out with.

LIZZIE: Belle, there's oul' Josie. Look at her standin' at the corner of the street shakin' her fist at us.

MARY: C'mon nigh, Herbie, the likes of you can afford more than a penny.

LORRIE: Did yous hear her? 'Yous don't know what hard work's like; away home til yer men'!!

LIZZIE: Oh! Thanks very much, missus. Support the strike!

BELLE: Oul' Josie? Wait'll yis hear this. Hey Josie, are y'still folleyin' the sailors down to the docks? Aha, that soon got rid of her!

FLORRIE: Hey you, c'mon now. I know ye; you're a foreman at the Rope Works, aren't ye? Aye well, you can afford more than that! Thanks very much!

LIZZIE: Here, where's Ethna McNamara? A quare geg she is. I haven't clapped eyes on her all day.

FLORRIE: Wee Ethna was round seein' me last night—one of her weeins is wile bad. That's why she's not here.

MARY: C'mon nigh! We're collectin' for the union!

BELLE: Here yousins, c'mon and get the dockers comin' out of work.

FLORRIE: And we're stayin' out to the bitter end.

LIZZIE: Belle, Belle, don't be doin' that. If Charlie sees me whe
he's comin' out of work, he'll have my life.

FLORRIE: C'mon you two.

BELLE: Don't worry, Lizzie. We'll hide ye. [*All exit except* MARY
BELLE *and* LEADPIPE *who is still drumming away.*] C'mo
Leadpipe, put a step in it.

MARY: If he cud talk, you'd be called some names, Bell
Thompson.

BELLE: If he talked the way he plays, he's as well shuttin' up.

They exit.

Scene 8

LIZZIE *and* CHARLIE *are sitting on a park bench. They are dressed
in their Sunday best.*

CHARLIE (Belle) [*shouting out front*]: Samuel, come away from
the edge. If y'fall in I'm not wettin' m'good Sunday best ti
get y'out.

LIZZIE: Do as your father says, Samuel, go on nigh and find the
other wans and give our heads peace.

CHARLIE: Gonna be a fine lad, young Samuel. If he keeps his
nose clean, I'm gonna speak til my superiors and see 'bout
gettin' him a wee office job.

LIZZIE: Our Samuel in an office, nigh wudn't we be the quare
wans. He's right and smart, y'know; ... takes after his father.

CHARLIE: Well, let's hope he doesn't turn out daft, like his
mother ... er ... no offence, Lizzie dear.

LIZZIE: I know what you mean.

[*Silence*]

CHARLIE: Aye, ye just went like an oul' sheep and fallied the rest of the weemin.

LIZZIE: What else cud I do, Charlie? I don't want til haft til take any truck from Belle Thompson or that Florrie Brown.

CHARLIE: Lizzie, love, it takes a brave woman til stick til what she believes in. You shud have walked on by them w'your head held high.

LIZZIE: I'm not sure what I believe in.

CHARLIE: Surely til God, y'don't believe that a crowd of weemin is gonna do anything, do ye?

LIZZIE: Sure, they seem dead determined and everything, Charlie.

CHARLIE: So is Miss Galway. She's tryin' til do her best for yis and yis are not givin' the woman a chance b'takin' affairs in til your own hands.

LIZZIE: You hear tell Miss Galway is doin' this for the weemin and that for the weemin but sure nothin' is happenin'. I've niver clapped eyes on her.

CHARLIE: That's 'cause she's not runnin' round the streets singin' and carryin' on and makin' an eejit of herself. That woman has dignity, Lizzie, dignity.

LIZZIE: I niver thought of that, Charlie. It's just that the weemin is more for this Connolly fella.

CHARLIE: Nigh, there's a boyo shud go back til where he belongs and keep his nose out of weemin's affairs.

LIZZIE: Sure last year, when you were on strike w'the dockers, I heard you bummin' and blowin' about him, what a great speaker he was; I even heard you quotin' him.

CHARLIE: So he was ... so he was, but he wasn't on his own. The men stud behind him til we got the bosses til shift.

LIZZIE: Sure, isn't that what the weemin is doin'?

CHARLIE: It's not what Miss Galway wants yis til do nigh, is it? [*Silence*] Well?

LIZZIE: No, but ...

CHARLIE: No buts, Lizzie ... one must not stand in the road of progress. You can only have one pilot steering the ship.

LIZZIE: But sure if the ship is not movin', d'ya not think we shud all get out our oars?

CHARLIE [*taken aback by* LIZZIE's *logic*]: A crowd of weemin cannot row a ship, Lizzie dear. Stick w'Miss Galway and you won't be led astray.

LIZZIE: Led astray?

CHARLIE [*looking furtively around, then whispering*]: Yer man Connolly is for the Home Rule business.

LIZZIE: What?

CHARLIE: We cud be sold down the river, Lizzie.

LIZZIE: I knew he was one of the other sort but b'God I didn't know that.

CHARLIE: Sure, what about his non-sectarian strike band? Catholics and Protestants playin' together in the one band! It's all a big plot!

LIZZIE: A plot!

CHARLIE: Shush woman, or we'll have the whole of Victoria Park round us. [*Looking round again*] It's a plot til git the Prods and Catholics under the wan banner; then, Lizzie dear, there is no hope for our wee childer. [*Shouts out front*] Samuel, Charles, James and the rest of yis, we're goin' home nigh.

LIZZIE [*disturbed*]: What do I do nigh, Charlie? ... I dunno whether I'm comin' or goin'.

CHARLIE: Get back til your work in the mornin'. Ye can't deprive your wee childer of a bite in their mouths. I can't be expected til carry on supportin' them on my wages alone. Sacrifices will haft til be made if ya don't. Soon we might not be able til afford our wee extras, like the Alhambra of a Saturday night or your herrin's of a Sunday. And like, I need the odd ounce of tobacco nigh and again, which, I might add, I have sacrificed this week. Many another man wud not take this business so light.

LIZZIE: You're an awful good man, Charlie ... Jis tell me what t'do nigh.

CHARLIE: Speak til the weemin. Get them til listen to Miss Galway. Keep them away from Connolly ... not just for me love, but for your wee childer and the rest of the weemin in Belfast.

LIZZIE: Might take a bit of time, Charlie. I don't wanna go back on me own. Belle wud gimme a hell of a slatin'.

CHARLIE: All right, Lizzie. But not long. I want you back at your frame b'next week.

LIZZIE: You're a very understanding man, Charlie. [*She places her hand on* CHARLIE'*s knee.*]

CHARLIE [*embarrassed*]: Quit that, woman!! ... [*They get up and look across the audience.*] Luk over there, Lizzie. See that? Biggest shipyard in the world, what built the Olympic and the unsinkable Titanic. What a ship, eh? ... See that over there, Lizzie? That is Ulster's finest sample of achievement—Harland & Wolff! [*He gazes starry-eyed over the water.*]

LIZZIE: Stap your day-dreamin' or we'll miss the evening service. [*She walks off singing* 'I Have an Anchor'.]

CHARLIE [*to the audience*]: See weemin? Ye don't bate them wi' that! [*He makes a fist.*] Ye bate them wi' that! [*He points to his head.*]

Scene 9

The noise of a crowd can be heard as FLORRIE *and* MARY *enter carrying placards.*

FLORRIE: There's a quare crowd here, all the same, Mary.

MARY: There isn't half—must be hundreds and hundreds!

LIZZIE [*entering*]: There's more here than I thought.

BELLE [*entering*]: Hi ya, girls.

FLORRIE: Hello, Belle.

BELLE: Hi ya, Sadie! How's Molly? God, Florrie, look at big Annie McCartney's banner!

FLORRIE: Name a'God! Yon's half her coal-house door!

[ETHNA *enters.*]

BELLE: Jasus, Ethna, you'd be late for your own funeral. Where were ye?

ETHNA: Where d'ye think? Up at the pawn.

BELLE: How much?

ETHNA: Sixims.

BELLE: What on?

ETHNA: His Ma's pilla-cases.

BELLE: Ach, that was awful good of her.

ETHNA: She doesn't know.

LIZZIE: What?! You pawned Maggie McNamara's pilla-cases and she doesn't know! Huh! There'll be murder when she finds out.

ETHNA: What do I care—it's to feed her grandchildren, isn't it?

MARY: What'll Alfie say?

ETHNA: It was him ordered me to do it.

BELLE: Jasus, what is this strike doin' to us, eh? Family stealin' off family.

ETHNA: I wudn't be worryin', Belle. First week I was married, I pawned two pairs of her drawers!

FLORRIE: There he is! That's him now.

MARY: Is that Connolly?

LIZZIE: Oh look, here's Miss Galway too.

BELLE: What's she doin' here?

FLORRIE: I think both of them's goin' to speak.

BELLE: Well I'm not listenin' to her.

LIZZIE: Well I am! I don't know what business it is of James Connolly to bother with the mill workers.

MARY: But sure nobody was payin' us any mind before this.

ETHNA: I don't know what all the fuss is about.

BELLE: He wants us to form our own union!

LIZZIE: Look, she's gettin' up nigh.

MARY: Is that her?

BELLE: Look at her. She's a bake on her that wud turn milk!

FLORRIE: I can't see her.

MARY: Over there by the gates.

FLORRIE: Oh aye, I can see her nigh.

ETHNA: Jasus, I think I owe her money!

LIZZIE: Shush! She's gettin' up to speak.

[*The pre-recorded voices of* GALWAY *and* CONNOLLY *are heard through the sound speakers.*]

GALWAY: As full-time Secretary of the Society of Textile Workers, I'm here to address you, the women of York Street Mill, concerning the present unrest at your place of work. First of all, let me say that I'm in total sympathy with you. But the question we must ask ourselves is: 'Are we doing this the right way? Is striking the only answer?' Girls, I think not. As a full-time trade union worker, I'm advising you to go back to work in the meantime and I will represent you.

CONNOLLY: Fellow workers. First of all, let me offer you my personal congratulations on your courageous decision to embark on an all out strike at York Street Mill. As a worker

I know that it's not an easy decision to strike. But once you show yourselves in earnest about your demands, sisters and fellow workers, demonstrate your intention to stick together and stay out til the bitter end, then victory is well within your grasp.

GALWAY: Don't put your jobs in jeopardy. Act wisely and open negotiations with the masters.

CONNOLLY: Don't be frightened by the timid counsels and fears of weaklings.

GALWAY: Girls, take no heed of themins that has nothing to do with our mills or even our city.

CONNOLLY: Be brave, sisters! Have confidence in yourselves.

GALWAY: This wild strike action can't succeed.

CONNOLLY: Talk about success and you will achieve success.

GALWAY: Mr Connolly is an extremist and a Home Ruler.

CONNOLLY: Go forth from here today and organise a union for yourselves. Remember, the linen mills of Belfast won't produce a single tablecloth without you. Stick at it, and good luck!

[*The women cheer.*]

BELLE: Well, girls, do we need to hear anymore?

ALL: No!

BELLE: Are we stayin' out?

ALL: Aye!

[*They all exit, except for* LIZZIE, *singing.*]

    Oul' Bingham thought he had us with his rules and cuts,
    Oul' Bingham thought he had us with his rules and cuts,
    Oul' Bingham thought he had us, but you see
        he didn't get us,
    With his rules, rules, rules and cuts.

LIZZIE [*scornfully*]: Some people wud be led by the nose!

Blackout

ACT II

Scene 1

The cast, dressed as men, with orange-and-green sashes, erupt onstage as the non-sectarian strike band. They make several remarks to each other (e.g. 'Hey Georgie, get it right this time. Don't be letting the side down.'/'It's not me, Billy; it's the Catholics. They've no sense of rhythm.) The band master restores order with 'Band, band! By the left, mark time!' Everyone marks time and shouts 'left' as they step on the left. They begin the tune 'My Aunt Jane' and march around the stage. Then exit.

ETHNA [*entering, shakes a collection box*]: Support the strack and save me and me wee childer from the workhouse. Hey, Mrs McKee, 'member the time I loaned you my Alfie to fix your scullery door. Put a penny in for Mr Connolly's strack fund.

VOICE [*offstage*]: Away t'hell, Ethna. I'm not givin' no money t'keep that drunken pig of a man of yours up in whiskey.

[*The others enter.*]

FLORRIE: How much did y'get, Ethna?

ETHNA: About two and tuppence halfpenny!

BELLE: Two and tuppence halfpenny! That's great Ethna.

MARY: Who gave?

ETHNA: Wee Mrs McCracken, big Patsy from the stick yard and Alfie's Ma.

BELLE [*grabbing box*]: That's great, Ethna ... Ethna, this box is empty.

LIZZIE: What happened t'the money, Ethna?

ETHNA: Well, there wud have been two and tuppence halfpenny.

LIZZIE: Wha'd'ya mean, wud've been?

ETHNA: Well, they said to support the strike with the money I owed them!

BELLE [*exiting*]: I'm away over to the Union Rooms to get this week's strike money. I'll be back in a minute.

[*The women begin to picket—walking around the stage with placards.*]

MARY: Y'know this doesn't make sense to me at all. We came out on strike 'cause they were cuttin' our hours and our money. Luk at us nigh, all we're doin' is walkin' round in circles and for next t'nothin'.

LIZZIE: Aye, nigh yer talkin', Mary. A lot of good walkin' round in circles is doin' us. There's wiser in the lunatic asylum.

ETHNA: Can we stop soon; my head's gettin' light?

LIZZIE: Y'know, Mary, every day I'm waitin' on a note comin' round from that mill tellin' me not to come back. A hell of a lot a' good runnin' round the streets with bits a wood will do us if we lose our jobs.

MARY: Ach, they wudn't do that to us, wud they? Florrie, do you think they wud? [FLORRIE *doesn't reply.*] I'd be first to go. Jim Doran hates me. He'd put word round the rest of the mills and I'd never get a job.

ETHNA: It'll be all right, Mary. Belle says he's bound to give in.

LIZZIE: Ach, Belle says this, Belle says that. If Belle stuck her head in the fire wud you stick yours in too, Ethna McNamara?

ETHNA: Yes, I wud!

FLORRIE: Ach wud yis for God's sake quit bickerin'. Swear to God tryin' to organise yous weemin's like tryin' to round up a herd of cattle! Luk, Lizzie, what we're tryin' to do is a bit like tryin' to move a mountain when you've only got a spoon to dig it with. I know it's goin' to be slow but we will get there in the end if we persevere and I do mean all of us. Lizzie, luk at what we've done already. We have Catholics and Protestants dancin' up and down together. They're playing' together in the wan band! And for what? So's that when our Susie or Ethna's weeins or even your wee childer, when they go into that mill, they'll have a decent livin'.

BELLE [*entering with a tin of money*]: Jasus, I can't leave yis for two minutes but yis are like a pack of gravediggers. Cheer up, everybody, it's pay day!

[*The women crowd round as* BELLE *counts out their money.*]

ETHNA: How much did we get, Belle?

BELLE: Two shillings each!

LIZZIE: Two shillings. Well, I suppose it cud've bin worse.

FLORRIE: Aye Lizzie, it cud've bin nothin'!

BELLE: Lizzie bin cheerin' everybody up again?

LIZZIE: Ah, go to blazes, Belle!

MARY [*receiving her share*]: Just thinkin' Belle; we must've collected a quare lot if every single woman out on strike got two bob each.

ETHNA: That's hundreds and hundreds a' pounds.

FLORRIE: Cud I have mine in pennies, Belle? It always makes you feel y'have more.

ETHNA: Where's mine, Belle?

BELLE: Oh aye, that's right, Ethna. I've a wee message for you.

ETHNA: For me! Who from?

BELLE: Mr Connolly himself. He said, 'Tell Ethna McNamara she's been such a good union supporter she can have a raise.'

ETHNA: A raise? Me? Honest to God, Belle?!

BELLE: Instead of two shillings, you can have two and tuppence halfpenny. [*She hands* ETHNA *her empty box back. Everyone else leaves.* BELLE *hands* ETHNA *two shillings.*] Mr Connolly says he'll loan you that til next week.

ETHNA: Belle Thompson, you're gettin' worse. Between you and Humpy Hessie, you've my heart broke!

Scene 2

The cast sing 'These Three Drunken Maidens' *while changing into costumes (hats and scarves).* MARY *and* LIZZIE *exit.*

CHARLIE: C'mon, Leadpipe, it's your round.

[LEADPIPE *indicates it is* BISCUIT'*s round.*]

BISCUIT (Ethna): All right, all right. [*He rises.*] Leadpipe, loan us sixims. [LEADPIPE *refuses.*] Nigh, I'm a peace-lovin' man. I don't want to start a row. [LEADPIPE *hands over the money.* BISCUIT *hands it back.*] Nigh, go and get the drink. [LEADPIPE *goes to exit.*] Oh, and Leadpipe ... keep the change.

[*The men all laugh and* LEADPIPE *exits.*]

CHARLIE: Leadpipe's rakin' a wee fortune playin' for the non-sectarian strike band. He even supports the women's wee strike.

BISCUIT: He what?!

HENRY (Florrie): Well, why shudn't he, hey? Them women's every right to strike. I toul my Belle: y'get nowhere sittin' on yer arse. It's about time them women took a leaf outta the dockers' book, eh Charlie?

BISCUIT: Know what's wrong with you, Henry, you're too soft. See my Sadie, she's gonna get that! [*He smacks his fist into the palm of his hand.*]

CHARLIE: Nigh, steady on, Biscuit. If you use the right approach with women, there's no need to bate them.

BISCUIT [*shouts*]: C'mon, Leadpipe, put Ginny down. I'm dyin' a thirst out here.

[GINNY *and* LEADPIPE *enter.*]

GINNY: C'mon nigh, yousins, it's closin' time. You'll have the polis in on top of me.

[*She collects their bottles. The men all protest vigorously.* CHARLIE *calms them.*]

CHARLIE: Hey ... a ... Ginny ... how's about a drink for Charlie here?

GINNY [*chucking him under his chin*]: Oooh you! [*She exits.*]

HENRY: Hey! Charlie boy, you're well in there, oul' son.

CHARLIE: Lads, did you see the way Ginny looked at me?

HENRY: Did I what?!

BISCUIT: Better not let your Lizzie find out!

HENRY: There'd be ructions, ructions.

CHARLIE: Girl like that makes my Lizzie look like a man!

[*Knocking is heard offstage.* GINNY *enters.*]

GINNY: Clear aff, we're shut!

ALFIE (Lizzie) [*offstage*]: It's Alfie McNamara, Ginny. I've a message for Charlie McCormick and themins.

GINNY: Aye well all right then, but no drink mind.

[GINNY *exits.* ALFIE *enters.*]

HENRY: What about ye, Alfie son?

CHARLIE: Alfie!

BISCUIT: Alfie!

ALFIE: Themins up at Blackstaff and Jennymount's all away back the morra. That means that from the morra onwards our weemin's the only weemin still out on strike.

HENRY: Well, they shud've stuck it out. Only a few more days they'd've had them mill owners eating out of their hands.

BISCUIT: Strikin' is for men. See weemin, see my Sadie, she's gonna get that. [*He smacks his fist into the palm of his hand again.*]

CHARLIE: I toul my Lizzie she was wastin' her time. Ye see talkin' to weemin, Alfie, it's like talkin' to that wall.

ALFIE: Ya don't talk to weemin, Charlie. A good hidin's the only medicine my Ethna knows. See weemin, they shudn't be allowed out on strike.

BISCUIT: Out on strike! They shudn't be allowed outta the house!

CHARLIE: You mark my words, Biscuit, soon the weemin's not gonna want to work at all.

ALFIE: God!

HENRY: Am I listenin' to the same men that big Jim Larkin had bringin' this city til its knees in the dockers' strike? Why don't you support your weemin and not the mill owners?

ALFIE: Ah give my head peace, Henry. Weemin's only good for one thing ... or maybe Belle's past it?

[*There is silence as* HENRY *rises to his feet.*]

HENRY [*exiting*]: Yous are like a wean of childer.

BISCUIT: Know what's wrong with him? He's heart feared a Belle. See my Sadie, see that? [*Looking at his fist*] No bother!

SADIE (Mary) [*offstage*]: Is that Biscuit one there?

HENRY [*offstage*]: Aye Sadie love, Biscuit's here all right, but you'd better watch yourself. He says he's gonna bate ye.

SADIE [*entering*]: Oh, is he nigh? We'll soon see about that! Where is the ghett?

CHARLIE: Now easy on, Biscuit son. I don't want you batin' Sadie in here. Ginny's just had the place fixed up.

BISCUIT: Ah it wasn't me, love. Charlie there got me drunk. I'm sorry, love.

SADIE: Ah get home, you no-good ghett ye. The childer's running wild in the streets.

BISCUIT: I'm sorry love.

SADIE [*grabbing* BISCUIT *and manhandling him out the door*]: Ah, wait'll I get you home!

CHARLIE: See that, Alfie? Men like him is givin' us a bad name!

Scene 3

The first four lines of 'These Three Drunken Maidens' *are sung while the cast change their costumes.*

ETHNA *is standing in a pool of light. She mimes knocking at doors; as each door is knocked, there are different responses:*

VOICE 1: Ye must be jokin', love! I'm just after givin' a wee girl for the strike.

VOICE 2: You're comin' at a bad time, but here's a penny anyway.

VOICE 3: That sounds bad right enough, love; here take this thruppence, an' I hope she soon gets better.

VOICE 4: Ach, Ethna, are ye lukin' the three and six for the doctor? Here's a penny anyway.

VOICE 5: Mammy's not in.

ALL: Go away, Ethna.

Scene 4

CHILD'S VOICE [*shouting offstage*]: Florrie, Susie's hitting me!

FLORRIE [*offstage*]: In the name of God, Thomas, stop that! Susie put that down!

SUSIE [*offstage*]: Florrie, I want my tea.

FLORRIE [*offstage*]: Yer tea? You had your tea over half-an-hour ago, now give over. Jesus, Thomas, I warned you! [*A slap is heard.* THOMAS *screams.* SUSIE *continues to shout about her tea.* FLORRIE *entering*] I swear to God, Susie, if you don't shut up I'll give you what Thomas got.

BELLE [*entering*]: In the name of God, what's goin' on here? You'd think there was a boxin' match up at the Chapel fields.

FLORRIE: It's them friggin' children!

BELLE: You annoyin' them weeins again?

FLORRIE: Me annoyin' them?! Christ, they'll have me in the madhouse before I'm finished. I swear to God, Belle, I've never seen a wee girl like thon Susie one—that girns as much as she does. It's drivin' me to distraction.

BELLE: Ach, Florrie, you're takin' it too much to heart.

FLORRIE: What am I supposed to do, Belle? Let them run wild altogether?

BELLE: It's this oul' strike. It's gettin' to ye.

FLORRIE: No, it's not.

BELLE: But don't you worry, Florrie, you're not on your own. There's my wee Robert—I had to put him to bed early. He hadn't a shoe on his feet and you know what their wee feet's gettin' this weather. Oh aye, it's the strike all right. It's just not that easy to live on two shillings a week.

FLORRIE: Ah well, at least most of yous has yer men's money comin' in.

BELLE: Aye well, don't you worry Florrie; it'll not be long before oul' Bingham's comin' into our wee kitchens beggin' us to go back to work.

FLORRIE: Ach, Belle, we've been out on strike near a week and he hasn't as much as budged!

BELLE: Aye well, I wudn't bet two pig's feet on that.

LIZZIE [*entering*]: Florrie! Florrie! Oh ... hi ya, Belle. Florrie, Mary Galway's only after tellin' me that all the ones up at Blackstaff and the ones up at Jennymount too—they're all goin' back the morra.

BELLE: Are you sure?

FLORRIE: Were you talkin' to Mary Galway herself?

LIZZIE: Aye. Sure, she came round to the house to tell me.

BELLE: Oh God, you and her's quare and great!

LIZZIE: She says she was up and spoke to them outside their mills and they all agreed to go back and let her negotiate.

BELLE: I'd luk sick!

LIZZIE: Well, we cud hardly stay out nigh!

FLORRIE: I heard this mornin' that this strike was spreadin' down as far as Greencastle.

BELLE: Oh aye, the strike's still all right, Florrie.

LIZZIE: How cud it be when the ones that came out with us is goin' back the morra?

BELLE: Ach, for God's sake Lizzie!

FLORRIE: Well, we'll have to have a meetin'. We'll have it in your house after supper, Lizzie.

LIZZIE: Oh dear no! Well, he'd be in and anyway I go out of a Tuesday. I go to our Annie's.

BELLE: There's a strike on, Lizzie.

LIZZIE: Not for much longer as far as I can see, Belle. Accordin' to Mary Galway, they're all goin' back the morra and if you want my opinion, I think you shud be grateful that Mr Bingham will have us back.

BELLE: Oh God aye! Thanks Mr Bingham, thanks for lettin' me slave twelve hours a day, up to me ankles in water, up to me eyeballs in pouce and smellin' like the arsehole of a donkey! Thanks Mr Bingham, for lettin' me breathe and go to the toilet!

LIZZIE: Aye, well, I'll go on nigh. The childer'll be starvin' with hunger. Do yis want me to tell Mary Galway anything?

BELLE: Aye, tell her to frig aff and mind her own business! Mary friggin' Galway!

[LIZZIE *exits.*]

FLORRIE: Well, we are goin' to have to have a meetin', Belle. It'll have to be here. If what she says is true and they are goin' back to work, there's goin' to be ructions among our girls. Some of them might want to go back to work too—maybe all of them.

SUSIE [*offstage*]: Florrie! Thomas is tryin' to push me off the yard wall!

FLORRIE [*rising*]: In the name of Christ!

BELLE [*stopping her*]: Florrie, y'know what we shud do? We'll get the women organised and we'll run a wee charabanc.

FLORRIE: A what?

BELLE: A charabanc. The weemin needs cheered up. I'll go and ask Connolly to give me money outta the strike fund. We'll run a charabanc.

SUSIE [*offstage*]: Florrie! Thomas is hittin' me!

FLORRIE: A charabanc! Aw, Belle, for frigs sake!

Scene 5

ETHNA *is standing in a pool of light.*

ETHNA: Oh Charlie, it's you. Is Lizzie in? I'm ... lukin' somethin' to put towards the three and six for the doctor. It's the chile, she's not a bit well.

CHARLIE [*offstage*]: Lizzie is not in ... but I toul her til tell you weemin you're wastin' your time.

ETHNA: I just need about one or two pennies ...

CHARLIE: If you'd listen less to that Connolly fella and more to Miss Galway ...

ETHNA: But Mr Connolly ...

[CHARLIE *continues to lecture* ETHNA. *She interrupts, pleading for some money.*]

CHARLIE: I toul my Lizzie ...

ETHNA: It's all right, Charlie ...

CHARLIE: We're all goin' to be sold down the river, Ethna.

ETHNA: I ... I'll ... come back the morra.

She exits. Link music for URSULA's *drawing room.*

Scene 6

Drawing room of URSULA BINGHAM'S *home.* MYRTLE (LIZZIE) *is seated at an imaginary piano;* URSULA *is talking on the telephone.*

URSULA (Belle): Hello ... oh, hello Margaret ... How are you? ... Oh, don't be talking ... family tensions, Margaret, family tensions. Oh Eric's bearing up, Margaret, bearing up. No, he's out at the moment, Margaret. He's at the monthly

meeting of the Board of Guardians ... Yes, I'll tell him. How's
your mother? ... and Norman? ... Oh, good, good!

ELIZABETH (Mary) [*offstage*]: Yoo, hoo! We're here, Ursula.

URSULA: In the drawing room, ladies. Oh, excuse me Margaret,
I must dash ... Yes, goodbye.

[*The ladies enter.*]

ELIZABETH: Good morning Ursula, how are you? How's Eric?
Bearing up under the strain?

URSULA: Oh don't be talking, Elizabeth, family tensions, family
tensions. Excuse me, ladies. [*She shouts offstage.*] Dolly,
Dolly! We'll serve tea in the morning room after our
rehearsal. [*She goes to greet* AMY.]

AMY (Ethna): New maid, Ursula?

URSULA: Yes. She's a sweet child. Eric brought her up from the
workhouse. The Board of Guardians are doing a great job
rehabilitating the poor. [*She greets* LYDIA.]

ELIZABETH: The workhouse? That was risky.

URSULA [*arranging the three ladies in their poses*]: Well, you know
one must take chances for the sake of charity. The only
problem is ... she'd had a child ... and a drink problem. We
just have to keep an eye on her.

LYDIA (Florrie): Well, I did bring some of my poetry as you
suggested, Ursula.

URSULA: Yes, later Lydia, later. Gilbert & Sullivan is first on the
priority. Yes, that's pretty. Oh try and look coy for goodness
sake, Lydia! That's better. Now ladies, let's have one good
bash at this—and I don't need to remind you that the Board
of Guardians' concert is on Friday—so buck up please.
Ready, Myrtle? Ready, ladies? One, two, three.

[*The telephone rings.*]

URSULA: Oh, fiddlesticks! Now ladies, don't move a muscle!
Hello! Oh, hello Eric! Oh Eric, I don't believe you; I don't

believe you, Eric ... It's shocking behaviour, Eric ... Disgraceful behaviour, Eric ... Yes, Eric ... I'll be here, Eric ... Goodbye, Eric. [*To the ladies*] That was Eric.

LYDIA: Is everything all right, Ursula?

URSULA: Those awful shawlies, they've written a sign up on York Street Mill wall—'Eric Bingham is a ... ' I can't even repeat the word.

ELIZABETH: Go and get Ursula a tot of brandy.

[LYDIA *does so.* ELIZABETH *and* AMY *go to* URSULA.]

URSULA: You house them, you give them a living, try to get them out of their slum-ridden conditions by providing work for them. Those ... those ... bitches!

[URSULA *is handed the brandy.*]

AMY: Calm down, Ursula, there, there. My husband says drink is the root of their problem. The sooner he and the Reverend Yates and the 'Catch Me Pal' Society get those dens of evil closed, the better! ... We're going to get them to sign pledges.

LYDIA: Well, I've always thought that if they had some of the finer things in life—take their minds off striking ... some Gilbert & Sullivan, perhaps ... some poetry ... some of the lighter, more romantic poets. I feel ...

URSULA: Oh do shut up, Lydia! I'm sorry, but we must proceed. [LYDIA *hands the remainder of her drink to* URSULA, *who in turn hands it to* MYRTLE, *who downs it in one. The ladies re-position themselves.*] Do you know what I'm going to tell you? It's that trouble-maker Connolly who's behind all this. He should go back to the Pike-Throwers in the bogs of Mayo—the people he's better suited to disrupt!

LYDIA: He is a very sincere man, Ursula.

URSULA: So was ... Jack the Ripper! Now, heads up ladies, and remember—feel the music of Gilbert & Sullivan—honesty is the essence of any performance. Ready, Myrtle? Ready, ladies? One, two, three, four.

They sing 'Three Little Maids from School' *and gradually, one by one, change to* 'Riding on a Tramcar'. *The scene is set for the Charabanc during the singing of* 'Riding on a Tramcar'. *By the end of the chorus they are seated and are thrown forward as the bus halts.*

Scene 7

In the Charabanc.

BELLE: Jasus, m'drink!

LIZZIE: Was that driver drinkin'?

MARY: I'll be glad to get off this tram.

ETHNA: Is this Kircubbin? My bum's throbbin'.

LIZZIE: Belle, I think this is a waste of money; I still think it is a waste of money.

BELLE: Come on, we've enough left for wan wee round.

[*The women and* LEADPIPE *get off the bus and breathe in the fresh country air.*]

FLORRIE: Aw, just look at that.

ETHNA: Hey Mary, luk at all the cows.

BELLE: Right girls, into the pub!

FLORRIE: You're drunk, Belle Thompson.

BELLE: Hand up til God, Florrie, sure I've only had five bottles of porter!

ETHNA: Hey Belle, I've none left!

BELLE: What are you lukin' at me for?

CHARABANC

"THE FIRST EXCURSION"

Destination - Belfast of 1911
when the city shuddered
to the sound of the looms
and the whir of the spindles

SOUVENIR   **PROGRAMME**

The front cover of the programme for the opening night of *Lay Up Your Ends* on 15th May 1983 at the Belfast Civic Arts Theatre.

l-r Carol Moore (Ethna); Brenda Winter (Lizzie); Marie Jones (Belle); Eleanor Methven (Florrie) on the charabanc outing.

Brenda Winter (Myrtle) 'playing' an accompaniment to 'Three Little Maids from School' for the Cleaver Ladies' Guild.

l-r Marie Jones (Belle); Dai Jenkins (Leadpipe).

l-r Carol Moore (Biscuit); Marie Jones (Charlie); Brenda Winter (Alfie) as the husbands discussing their wives going back to work

Marie Jones (Belle) *right* confronts the spinning master, Doran, (Carol Moore) *left*.

l-r Marie Jones (Belle); Eleanor Methven (Florrie) address the striking mill workers.

Brenda Winter as the mill boss, Eric Bingham.

Carol Moore
(Biscuit).

Eleanor Methven (Florrie).

Belle (Marie Jones) *right* comforts Mary (Maureen Macauley) *left* over her suspension.

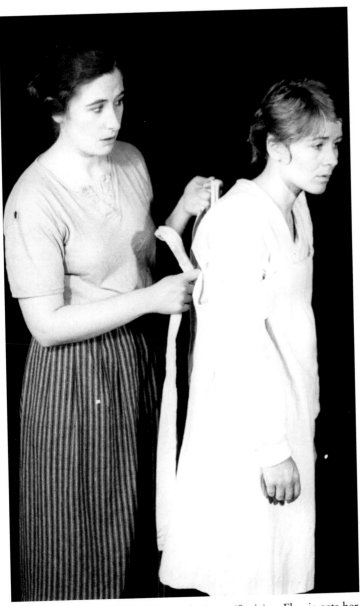

l-r Eleanor Methven (Florrie); Carol Moore (Susie) as Florrie gets her young sister ready for school.

During rehearsal: l-r *sitting* Brenda Winter; Marie Jones; Eleanor Methven; Maureen Macauley *standing behind* Dai Jenkins and Aidan McCann

During rehearsal: Carol Moore *left* and Marie Jones *right* discussing the script with Martin Lynch.

l-r (sitting) Aidan McCann; Brenda Winter; Eleanor Methven; Maureen Macauley; (kneeling) Marie Jones and Carol Moore.

Russian trip: Pam Brighton in conversation on board the train to Vilnius.

STORY LINE (FLORRIE)

① MODERN FACTORY SCENE Lighting + Siren etc

SONG 1.

Linked | to (Machine sound
Dai's balls/colour
Florrie and wiping down incident)

② FIRST 1911 MILL SCENE SONG 2.

○ [Florrie introduces herself here.]

Belle is in to baby-sit. The kids are shouting down the stairs placing various demands on FLORRIE

③ ANOTHER FLORRIE SCENE

Ⅳ MILL SCENE — NOTICES
DISCONTENTMENT
FLORRIE GETTING MARRIED   INCIDENT
TOILETS

SONG

At end of scene Mary talks of unions

(Possible scene in street)

Ⅴ CUSTOM HOUSE STEPS.

They hear CONNOLLY
BELLE IS CONVINCED

Two dummies (Dai & Pauline.)

SONG

Part of a rough storyline used by the company to plan and structure the scenes.

The entire company in a publicity shot outside Ross's mill. Far left are Martin Lynch and Ian McElhinney.

Inside a linen mill; one of the cleaner parts of the process.

The 'B' team: for further details see Martin Lynch's account of the Russian trip!

Flowers, applause and plaudits after a performance in Moscow.

l-r Maureen Macauley (Mary) and Brenda Winter (Lizzie) on the Russian tour with the strike signs in Russian.

l-r Aidan McCann; Marie Jones; Eleanor Methven; Carol Moore; Brenda Winter; Maureen Macauley and Pam Brighton in Red Square.

Acknowledgements

Mrs. Florrie Banks

Mrs. Nellie Brown

Mrs. Sarah Christie

Mrs. Kathleen Conlon

Mrs. Kitty Erwine

Mrs. Bella Ferrie

Mrs. MacLachlan

Mrs. Sarah Magowan

Mrs. Elizabeth Marshall

Mrs. Bella O'Hara

Mary O'Hare

Mrs. Mary O'Neill

Miss Sadie Patterson

Doctor Mary Paulin

Mrs. Annie Quinn

Mrs. Elizabeth Simms

Mrs. Annie Sommerville

Mrs. Emily Stephenson

Mrs. Anna Winter

Julie Barber

Jonathan Bardon

Paddy Devlin

Carmel Gallagher

Pat Hill

Maurice Leyden

Lady McDermot

Mr. Christie (Ulster Folk Museum) John O'Hara

Sheila Speers (Ulster Museum) Terry De Winne

John Gray (Linenhall Library) Jim White

Mr. Montgomery (Lambeg Industrial Research Centre)

Trevor Parkhall (Public Records Office)

Mervyn Elder (Leisure Services)

Brendan Henry, Brian Morrison (Community Services)

Belfast Civil Arts Theatre

Tyrone Guthrie Centre

Belfast Central Library

Bernard and Mary Loughlin

Rev. and Mrs. McElhinney

Cantrell & Cochrane   Jackie Hewitt (Farsett Youth Project)

Mr. Larmour, Mr. Scott (Ulster Weaving Co. & Killyleagh Spinning Co.)

B.B.C. for use of Sound Tapes

Charabanc Theatre Company gratefully acknowledges financial support of Action for Community Employment and Belfast City Council.

ETHNA: Gimme some of yours.

BELLE: Aye ... Hi ya, Burke.

ETHNA: You owe me a cabbage and four potatoes from last week.

BELLE: Here! [*She hands* ETHNA *her bottle.*] If you can get a cabbage and four potatoes out of that, I'll go til Mass with you on Sunday! [*Turning away from the others*] I wonder how many went in this morning? [*Snaps her bottle back*] C'mon into the pub. C'mon, Leadpipe til ... lay up your ends!

[MARY *and* LIZZIE *re-enter.*]

MARY: Except the pub's closed!

BELLE: What!?

MARY: A man's after tellin' us it won't be open for another hour.

LIZZIE [*accusingly*]: There was a death in the family.

BELLE: Wha'd'ya lukin' at me for? I didn't kill him!

LIZZIE: What are we gonna do until the pub opens?

BELLE: Jasus, there's no pleasin' some people! Lizzie, luk around you ... trees, fields, grass, even a wee river over there ... Cheer up! You cud be sittin' at home lukin' at Charlie! Hey girls, did I ever tell yis the wan about the country man who comes up to Belfast for the day?

FLORRIE: No.

BELLE: Well, he went into Robinson's Hotel and ordered the biggest beef steak they had.

LIZZIE: Well seein' he didn't work in the mill.

BELLE: Says the waiter, 'Do ye want it under done, medium done or well done?' Says he, [*Imitating a country accent*] 'No, I dinee want nothin' fancy. Just pull off its horns, wipe its arse and buck it on the plate.'

[*They all laugh.*]

ETHNA: Sure did you not hear about the time I was lyin' bad?

MARY: You're always bad, Ethna, but you won't lie down.

ETHNA: No, this is true. The other week I was lyin' awful bad when my Ma called round. She came upstairs, tuck one luk at me and went straight down to him. She was very concerned like. I wasn't one bit well. She says til him, 'I don't like the luk of my Ethna.' Says he, 'Neither do I, but she's good to the kids'. [*They all laugh.*] That is the God's truth.

LIZZIE: I feel sick.

FLORRIE: I told you to watch your drink.

LIZZIE: I wonder how many went through them York Street gates this mornin'?

FLORRIE: There's still a majority out.

BELLE: Aye. Didn't Annie McBurney go in yesterday and came straight back out at dinner hour with fourteen others?

LIZZIE: Fourteen, Belle! The weemin's been goin' back in their hundreds practically since Monday! We're not even in a majority now.

FLORRIE: I'm sure we are. Sure there was over eight hundred at St Mary's Hall last night when Connolly spoke.

LIZZIE: We came out with near two thousand.

BELLE: Well, I wudn't care if I was left on m'own, I'm not goin' back! [*There is an awkward silence.*] Ah for Jasus sake, Lizzie, cheer up! Here, take a drink.

[LIZZIE *takes the bottle.*]

MARY: Here, I know, come on and we'll do a wee concert. Who wants to do a wee concert? Belle? Belle, wud ye?

BELLE: Frig ... she's aff again! Every week it's somethin' different. Last week she wanted to be like Marie Lloyd; the week afore that it was a dancer from London. Every time she goes to that Empire it's somethin' different.

LIZZIE: Your head's in the clouds, Mary dear.

MARY: Well, I don't wanna spend the rest of m'days in York Street Mill.

ETHNA: I'll do it with ye, Mary.

MARY [*disheartened*]: Aye, all right, Ethna.

[*They move upstage.* BELLE, LIZZIE *and* FLORRIE *are seated on grass centre stage.*]

LIZZIE: Thanks very much, Belle. That was very nice. You know I like a wee drink but he barges me for it in the house.

FLORRIE: Ah, let him run on there. You're only gonna nurse— you're not an invalid nor nothin'.

BELLE: Hey Lizzie, y'wanna know how you get twins?

LIZZIE: How?

BELLE: Sew a shirt button on the end of it! [LIZZIE *thinks; then sniggers.*] Ach Florrie, are we shamin' you? Us oul' married weemin. Like, we forget that you're not ... well, what I mean is, because you're older you wud think that ye shud ... er ... em ... What I mean is, you're wan of us ... but you're not, if you see what I mean ... em ... now that's not your fault, Florrie love.

LIZZIE: Ach no, it's not your fault, Florrie. Sure I know others ... sure there's oul' Josie never got nobody. It's not your fault, Florrie.

BELLE: Just the way your man up there planned it. 'Cause it's not 'cause Florrie's odd-lukin' or nothin', is it Lizzie?

LIZZIE: Ach, no.

FLORRIE: I did have a man once, y'know.

LIZZIE [*surprised*]: Y'did! Tell us about him, Florrie. What was he like?

MARY: Nigh Ethna, ye have to pretend it's night time, right?

ETHNA: Right, it's night time, dead dark and everything.

MARY: And you have to pretend you're creepin' round ...

ETHNA: What time of night is it, Mary? Like was it very late, or just late?

MARY: It doesn't matter what time it was, Ethna, ye just pretend.

ETHNA: Right, we're just goin' to pretend it's night time—about nine o'clock?

LIZZIE: What happened til him, Florrie?

FLORRIE: Well, he went off til America for til better himself.

BELLE: Why did you not go with him? See if it was me, I'd a bin on thon boat like a flyin' shuttle.

FLORRIE: How cud I go with all them weeins? No, I'll just have to put up with it. I'm on m'own, Belle, and no woman's a proper woman until she has a man to luk up til.

LIZZIE: Ach don't worry, Florrie. My Charlie will do any wee jobs round the house that need doin'.

BELLE: Look yous two, the only man worth lukin' up to is one that's about to jump off the Albert clock.

ETHNA: How do you pretend to be an owl, Mary?

MARY: Ach Ethna, it's easy; watch—towitt-towoo ... towitt-towoo.

ETHNA: Ach, for God's sake, Mary!

MARY: Ah, go on, Ethna—it's part of the play.

ETHNA: Towitt-towoo.

MARY: Pretend you're up a tree!

ETHNA: Up a tree, Mary?

FLORRIE: Y'know, sometimes I wish I was Mary. She's got Robbie and she has no cares. It's not fair, Lizzie.

LIZZIE: Ach now, Florrie, cheer up. Sure we'll not let ye get too miserable. If you're lonely any night, you can always come round and sit with Charlie and me. Nigh c'mon, we're all out here to enjoy ourselves.

ETHNA: Mary, what's the name of this wee play?

MARY: *Murder in the Red Barn*.

ETHNA: *Murder in the Red Barn*?

MARY: Nigh Ethna, you have to pretend to be the villain and stab me with a knife: nigh ...

ETHNA: I'm goin' to be the villain and I'm gonna stab you with ... What size was the knife, Mary?

MARY: It doesn't matter what size it is, just stick it in me, for Jasus' sake! [ETHNA *does as* MARY *asked.* MARY *screams. There is general consternation.*] That was very good, Ethna!

BELLE: Come on, Leadpipe son, give us a song—'Only a Bird in a Gilded Cage'.

[LEADPIPE *plays the introduction badly. They are all about to sing.*]

LIZZIE: Ach Belle, it's raining!

ETHNA: See you, Lizzie McCormick, you put a scud on things no matter where you go!

[*All except* BELLE *rush off to the charabanc.*]

FLORRIE: C'mon yousins, back to the charabanc. Harry put thon roof on.

[*The others make up the charabanc.*]

BELLE: Never mind the rain. Leadpipe, play on. [*She sings* 'Only a Bird in a Gilded Cage'.]

MARY: Come on Belle, you're gettin' soaked.

BELLE: Come on under m'shawl, Mary; you and me's quare chums, eh?

MARY: Aye, but I don't want to catch m'death, Belle.

BELLE: 'Mon back to the charabanc! [*They sit on the front two boxes. The others are asleep.*] Hey Mary, what does this wee fella, Rabbie, think of all this actin' carry on? [MARY *doesn't want to speak in front of the others.*] Ethna, do you want the loan of a shillin'? [*There is silence.*] It's all right; they're sleepin'.

MARY: He says once we're married it's up to me as long as I know what I'm doing.

BELLE: Do ye?

MARY: Won't know til I've done it.

BELLE: Aye, right enough.

MARY: I just know I don't wanna end up with a crowd of childer like the other wans.

BELLE: Jasus, I only had to take m'shoes off and I fell away!

MARY: Suppose I'll just haft to leave it in the lap of God.

BELLE: Or fall into money.

MARY: What has money got to do with it?

BELLE: Jasus, wudn't I love to know! Do you see wans that has plenty of money? They're not trippin' over twelve and thirteen childer, are they?

MARY: Maybe they don't do it as often. Maybe rich people is built different from us.

BELLE: Built different, m'arse! Belle just can't put her finger on it but d'y'see whatever it is, I wish t'God they'd tell us their secret. Then again, maybe we're not supposed to know.

MARY: Know what?

BELLE: Whatever it is.

MARY: Whatever what is?

BELLE [*pauses*]: Ah, for Jasus sake, Mary! [*She turns and goes to sleep.*]

MARY: Belle's always naggin' me. She says I'm always lukin' the happy-ever-after and it's time I stopped my day-dreamin'. She's worse than my mother! Well maybe I do dream a lot, but it's not all clouds in the sky. See me and my Robbie, I want to keep the feelin's I have for him. I get the head-staggers every time he touches my hand. I don't want us to end up like themins and their men, fightin' and arguin' and hatin' to lie together at night. Ach, my Robbie's sweet and good; he's different. I know he won't turn into one of them. But how come I got the only good wan? And how can love and all the nice things in life just ... ? Robbie's made me happier than I've ever been in my life and he was dead good over the strike and havin' to put aff the wedding, even though he's been goin' mad waitin' for me ... and I've been goin' mad waitin' for him too. Mind you, it was a great feelin', all the women together, just us, all agin the bosses. But it'll end soon, I know that. I feel sorry for Florrie and Belle and themins, 'cause they're dead sure and all, but you just know, don't ye? And then me and my Robbie'll get married.

[*The women sing* 'I'll Take you Home Again, Kathleen'. *The charabanc jolts to a halt. They get off.*]

LIZZIE: Here we are!

FLORRIE: That was a great day, Belle.

LIZZIE: It was a pity about the rain.

BELLE: See yis at the mill gates in the mornin'.

[LIZZIE, FLORRIE *and* BELLE *leave, shouting goodbyes.*]

ETHNA: Hey Mary ... Towitt-towoo! [*She laughs.*]

MARY: Towitt-towoo, Ethna! See ya in the morning. [*She exits laughing.* ETHNA *turns and bumps straight into* HUMPY HESSIE.]

HESSIE: Ethna McNamara, you were tryin' to juke me.

ETHNA: Jasus Hessie, m'heart! ... Ah ... I haven't got it to give you ... the strike ...

HESSIE: The strike nathin' ... I'm goin' round nigh to see your man.

ETHNA: He's ... am ... not in ... He's in the Glens a Gormley with his brother.

HESSIE: The Glens a nathin' ... I'm goin' round for m'money. [ETHNA *tries to stop her by grabbing onto her. Starting to hit* ETHNA] Leave me alone! You're tryin' to steal m'money!

ETHNA: I wasn't ... [ETHNA *is clearly upset.*]

HESSIE: I'll get the polis for ye. [*She becomes hysterical.*] I'm goin' round for your man.

ETHNA: Hessie ... wait ... please ... Wud you take three and six?

She takes money from her pocket. HESSIE *snatches the money from* ETHNA *and exits. As* ETHNA *turns to exit a voice sings,* 'I'll Take you Home Again, Kathleen'.

Scene 8

BELLE *and* LEADPIPE *enter carrying placards.*

BELLE: It'd fairly skin ye this mornin', hey Leadpipe? My feet's near froze off me. [LEADPIPE *mumbles in agreement unintelligibly.*] Hey you! Less of that talk! Hey Leadpipe, here they're comin'. [*She shouts*] Yous are playin' intil Bingham's hands, girls. Come on, Molly, if you stay out your girls will stick with ye ... Sadie, you've bin with us all along, you can't give in nigh ... [*To* LEADPIPE] She was the very one that said wild horses wudn't trail her over that gate ... Hey Sadie, if you stay out the rest of your girls will stick with ye. Do you not see—oul' Bingham's sittin' up there laughin' his leg off at us? Why has he got too much pilin' up in the warehouse, eh? ... 'Cause mugs like us have worked our fingers til the bone til put it there ... What thanks do we get, eh? Shorter hours ... less money ... and a list of rules and demands the length of your arm ... Girls, we're worth our weight in gold to these mill lords. Leadpipe ... d'ya think I'm wastin' m'breath ... ? It's hard to talk to these weemin' about what's right and fair when they've a clatter of starvin' weeins at home and maybe their man not workin' ... Luk at them, Leadpipe, trippin' over themselves til get in them gates ... If they were asked til go into that mill and work standin' on their heads, they'd do it ... I just cannot make them see what their worth is. [*She shouts*] Cissy McClurg, I've seen you and your girls layin' up a hundred ends like lightnin'. How could Bingham replace the likes of yous, eh?

FLORRIE [*entering*]: Well?

BELLE: Ach, they're near all in nigh, Florrie. Sure there's always the morra mornin', eh Leadpipe? [LEADPIPE *nods*.] Could ye not get nobody else to come out with ye this mornin'?

FLORRIE: Naw—themins that's still out on strike—ye can't get them outta their beds! Even big Annie McCartney. She says to me she thinks the strike is the quare oul' mark, sure she hasn't had a lie-in for nigh on fifteen years!

BELLE: We called round to see Ethna this mornin', Florrie. The wee chile's awful bad—took convulsions in the middle of the night—they're not expectin' her to last.

FLORRIE: Aye. It's terrible the way half the wee weans doesn't even get a chance.

[*The sound of the factory horn is heard.*]

BELLE: Look at that oul' Pinky Hewitt. You'd think it was the Pearly Gates, b'Jasus, he was shuttin'! Och, Florrie, look. There's oul' Minnie Harvey—she's late again. Hurry up, love—run—run! Let her in y'humpy oul' ghett! Sure as God, hell'll never be full til he's in it!

FLORRIE: We may go and put the points to Bingham again the morra, if he'll see us.

BELLE: Oh he'll see us all right—should I have to climb over them gates meself!

FLORRIE: Jasus Belle, don't be doin' that! Oul' Pinky Hewitt'll be lookin' up your clothes!

BELLE: Well if he sees anything he hasn't seen before—he can shoot it! By the way, where's that Mary Rooney one? She swore blind she'd be here.

FLORRIE: Och, sure her and Lizzie's thick as thieves these days ...

ETHNA *enters in tears and goes to* BELLE. *She and* FLORRIE *comfort her as they all exit.*

Link music (Gilbert & Sullivan). URSULA *and* ERIC BINGHAM *stroll on.* URSULA *has an imaginary dog on a lead.*

URSULA: Yes Eric, I think you can put your mind at rest now.

BINGHAM: You think so?

URSULA: Oh absolutely. I think the unrest is as good as over. You're down to ... what? ... three hundred die-hards, no strike money, no support in any art or part of the city—and the newspapers handled it really well, didn't they?

BINGHAM: Hardly a mention.

URSULA: Old George came up trumps again! No, I don't see why this should disrupt our winter holiday.

ERIC [*gazing out to the front*]: You know Ursula, Belfast is a fine city. Tough but prosperous, peaceful but industrious and it's ideally situated for commerce—the lough, the port, the hills. Yes—a fine city.

URSULA: It's a pity about the people!

BINGHAM: You know your trouble, Ursula ... you're too emotional.

URSULA: I am not!

BINGHAM: That's an Irish trait, you know.

URSULA: It is not ... I just don't see why we can't join Elizabeth and Sam in Paris on the date we said we would. I don't see why our winter holiday should be disrupted for this strike carry on.

BINGHAM: Well ... we'll see.

URSULA [*calling*]: Nip! Nip! Nip! [*To dog*] Heel! Heel! Did you do pooh-poohs? Good boy!

[*They stroll off.* LIZZIE *and* MARY *enter.*]

LIZZIE: No sign of the others?

MARY: I saw Florrie goin' into Belle's. They'll be here in a minute.

LIZZIE: Probably concoctin' some new reason for carryin' on with the strike.

MARY: You know Belle.

LIZZIE: Aye, only too well. D'you know Mary, that Belle Thompson one got me into trouble before. It was the time of the 1906 election—remember when wee Joe Devlin got elected? Well she started yellin' things at the polis and b'God they near arrested me! Charlie was goin' to kill me over the head of it.

MARY: Sounds like Belle all right!

LIZZIE: Aye she's an oul' eejit—but she's a big softy at heart.

[BELLE, ETHNA *and* FLORRIE *enter.*]

BELLE: Lizzie McCormick! What's this I hear about you goin' to Mary Galway behind our backs?

LIZZIE: What?

BELLE: We're tryin' to keep the women together and you're spreadin' rumours the strike's over!

LIZZIE: I only went for the woman's opinion.

BELLE: What for?

LIZZIE: Because I thought I would—that's what for! Belle, there hasn't been any strike money for days now and what there was you spent on that stupid charabanc!

BELLE: It doesn't matter, you'd ...

FLORRIE: Aye, all right Belle. We'll leave it for the minute.

BELLE: But Florrie, she'd no call to go ...

MARY: Aw for God's sake, Belle!

LIZZIE: It's two weeks now that yousuns have us out!

FLORRIE: *We*—have yous out!

LIZZIE: Well you must admit, Florrie, most of us was goin' by what you and Belle were sayin'.

FLORRIE: So the rest of you is just a crowd of sheep!

LIZZIE: Well, that's a bit strong!

BELLE: Crowd of bloody cowards, is more like!

LIZZIE: I'm no coward! I'm not afraid of anybody or anything in York Street Mill nor nobody else for that matter!

BELLE: Aye Lizzie, you'd shite coal brick so ye wud!

LIZZIE: Aye, that suits ye!

BELLE: Well I walked outta that mill and I'm not goin' back— not until we get what we want—James Connolly or no James Connolly!

MARY: We've got to go back.

FLORRIE: We have to do something, Belle.

BELLE: Aye—burn the place down!

FLORRIE: Och, that's stupid talk, Belle.

LIZZIE: What about you, Ethna? You haven't said anything yet.

ETHNA: I don't see any point.

LIZZIE: Nigh, there y'are. Even Ethna thinks we should go back.

ETHNA: I said I don't see any point. If we came out with nothin' what's the point in goin' back in with nothin'?

MARY: Aw, for frigs sake!

LIZZIE: You've wee childer!

ETHNA: So what? So what?! My weans were half-starved when we come out and they're half-starved nigh. It's not goin' to make any difference to them. If Eric Bingham wanted to starve us out, he hadn't far to go anyway.

LIZZIE: You'd your wages comin' in.

ETHNA: Aye, when they weren't takin' half them off me with fines.

FLORRIE: Right. Well, we put the points to Bingham again this morning and the only thing he's willin' to do is to take Mary Rooney back to work without any fines added on. But he's not goin' to give us Saturdays off with the shorter hours and he insists that the new rules that was put up by Jim Doran is oul' rules that has always been the rules of his firm. And from the time that York Street Mill first closed down there's now only seven hundred and eight people still out.

ETHNA: Only seven hundred?

FLORRIE: Well, as yous know, the rest of the mills went back after the first few days.

ETHNA: That's what was wrong, Belle—we were left out on our own.

MARY: And what's Connolly sayin'?

FLORRIE: Aye, well Belle and me disagrees about that, but he is sayin' we should go back to work.

LIZZIE: About time!

FLORRIE: He says he doesn't houl out much hope of Bingham givin' in with the shorter hours either and he's heard from across the water, in Lancashire like, they're goin' on shorter hours as well.

BELLE: This isn't Lancashire! This is Belfast!

FLORRIE: And his main point is there's not enough strike money to go round. No strike is goin' to succeed without some sort of financial back-up. But, on the other hand, he says we're now organised—it's only a matter of us going back in until we get a bit more support and then we'll be ready for Eric Bingham!

BELLE: And I say if we're not ready now, we'll never be ready!

MARY: Aw, for God's sake, Belle!

BELLE: What are you 'for God's sakin' Belle' for, Mary? I've a right to my opinion too, you know!

MARY: Well, there's no need to shove it down everybody else's throat!

BELLE: You have a bloody cheek! That's the thanks I get for stickin' up for ye!

MARY: Ye weren't stickin' up for me! My suspension had to end sometime; yous lot have us out two friggin' weeks now!

LIZZIE: It was somethin'.

ETHNA: Aye—somethin'.

FLORRIE: Belle, do you honestly think the rest of those weemin are goin' to stay out?

BELLE: I suppose not.

FLORRIE: Well neither do I!

BELLE: But I will!

FLORRIE: Look, we're goin' to haft til do what Connolly says!

MARY: All right, we're doin' what he says, but what about goin' back the morra?

FLORRIE: Well he says we're to go back to work, but not in ones and twos. We're all to gather together, outside the mill, in a body and all go in singin'!

ETHNA: Singin'?

FLORRIE: Aye, singin', because we're not supposed to be allowed to sing. Then, once we're inside, if one girl is reproved for talkin' at her frame, we all start talkin' together. If the like of Mary here gets toul off for laughin', we'll start laughin' too. And especially, if any girl is dismissed for breakin' any one of them rules, we're all out with her!

LIZZIE: Nigh that sounds more sensible.

MARY: That'd mean Jim Doran couldn't pick on any of us?

FLORRIE: What do yous all think? Belle?

BELLE: I don't want to go back, Florrie. I hate the bastards nigh. But, I suppose if we're all goin' to stick together, we may go in.

FLORRIE: Ethna?

LIZZIE: There's no point nigh, Ethna.

MARY: C'mon. We'll fight them at every turn.

FLORRIE: Oh aye. We're goin' to form our own union—to spake up for us in the future and Mr Connolly says he'll give us every help he can.

LIZZIE: Nigh that would be the first time we had one of those. I think you should be in charge of that, Florrie.

BELLE: What happened to Mary Galway?

LIZZIE: Aye, well ... Florrie's one of us!

FLORRIE: What do you think, Ethna?

ETHNA: I'm not goin' back to the mill, Florrie.

FLORRIE: Why?

ETHNA: Not goin' back near it—unless yous make me Doffin' Mistress.

[*The women laugh.*]

FLORRIE: Right look, Connolly says we have to go in singin'— what are we goin' to sing?

MARY: Somethin' bad about Jim Doran—somethin' about his hairy nose!

ETHNA: Aye! Somethin' about him scratchin' his arse—not to mention his itchy balls!

BELLE: Aye—cut them off him!

ETHNA: Oh nigh, I couldn't do that. You'd have me fined and I'd only be back. B'Jasus, I could do without another fine!

FLORRIE: Right, let's get the song made up. Which one'll we use?

[ETHNA *la-la's the tune of* 'Oul Bingham thought he had us' *and between them they arrive at the new version and exit singing.*]

Jim Doran thought he'd sack us
When we went on strike
Jim Doran thought he'd sack us
When we went on strike
Jim Doran thought he'd sack us
But y'see he didn't brack us
When we-went-out-on-strike!!!

Scene 10

In the mill. The noise of machinery can be heard. The women are working.

BELLE: Hey Florrie ... luk down there. Big Annie McCartney is standing in the middle of the pass combing her hair ... Jesus! They're all doin' it! ... Doran's seen them! ... Christ! He's goin' buck mad! He's lukin' down here!

[*The women gather centre stage and begin to comb their hair simultaneously.*]

ETHNA: Do yous hear him? [*Relaying and imitating* DORAN] 'Yous will all be sacked! ... Rule Number Four says "No adjusting hair while at work"!'

BELLE [*shouting back at* DORAN]: Away and shite!

ETHNA: 'You're sacked, Belle Thompson!'

FLORRIE [*at* DORAN]: You sack one; you sack us all!

ETHNA: 'And you, Florrie Brown!'

MARY: Then we'll all be out on strike again!

ETHNA: 'And you, Mary Rooney! Yous will all be sacked!'

BELLE [*starts to sing defiantly*]: 'You'd easy know a Doffer' ...

[*The women join in the song, one by one.* LIZZIE *continues to work at her machine.*]

FLORRIE [*stepping forward to address the audience*]: In November, 1911, just two weeks after those York Street Mill girls went back to work, the first branch of the Irish Transport and General Workers' Union was formed, especially for the Belfast mill-girls. Mary Johnston was appointed as its full-time secretary.

[FLORRIE *steps back into the line and the girls sing as they work. The noise of machinery comes up again.*]

Blackout

Original Programme Notes

Why This Play?

Martin Lynch

When I was first asked by a group of Belfast actresses to sit in on some discussions about a new play, I said, 'Yeah, ok, I'll go along.' But when it was further suggested that the new play should tour Belfast community centres, I immediately replied, 'Yeah, I'm definitely in.'

Community centres, as they say, is 'where I came in' seven short years ago when I wrote my first play for the Fellowship Community Theatre at Turf Lodge.

At the first meeting with the actresses I listened as they told me how they wanted me to write a play about the experience of Belfast women! The absurdity of this struck me immediately and I asked them why *they* couldn't sit down and write about their experiences as Belfast women. This produced an instant silence, followed by laughter.

Gradually they came round to the idea and it was agreed that we would write the play together.

But when we came to discuss the question, we realised that the women of today couldn't be viewed in isolation from the history of our own mothers and grand-mothers. Their experience, in many senses, made the Belfast women of today. What we wanted to do, we recognised, couldn't—or shouldn't—be done in one play. It would need perhaps a series of plays.

So how best to relate the history of the earlier Belfast woman?

Someone suggested that Belfast as a city reached its peak at the turn of the century, so why not start there? This was broadened to include the years from 1900 up to the beginning of the First World War. But then we felt this brief was too wide, we needed a focus, perhaps a particular female experience of the time.

In the course of the next month, as we held our weekly meetings and as the five actresses threw themselves head-first into the research of the period, it soon became apparent that the experience and struggle of the Belfast mill-girls stood head and shoulders above everything else.

Here were the headquarters of the largest linen mills in the world. Here were thousands of Belfast women, from eight to seventy years of age, toiling and sweating in the most atrocious non-unionised conditions to be found anywhere in Europe. Here was a story well worth telling and, bearing in mind the current attacks by the likes of Thatcher [British Prime Minister in 1983] and Tebbitt [a member of her government] on the very principle of organised Trade Unionism, the story would serve as a timely reminder to female (and male) workers of today, just why Trade Unions are vital and how exactly our parents and grandparents suffered and struggled in their time to make life that much more bearable for the working classes of today.

Belfast in 1911

Maureen Macauley

Belfast, a city dominated by respectability and success, faced the twentieth century with a sense of complacency. By 1911 it could boast not only the largest weaving and tobacco factories but also the largest output of shipping in the world. The 'Olympic', launched in 1910, was by far the biggest ship ever built and her sister ship, the 'Titanic', was to be even larger.

However, the Edwardian era was characterised by labour unrest as workers struggled to raise their standard of living. The gap between rich and poor yawned ever wider. Almost all the men of the upper class managed their own businesses and their wives rarely visited outside their own circle. Content with their sheltered existence, they regarded the working class as lazy, immoral and drunken. 'Saturday night,' said the Reverend Thomas Yates 'closes on a Belfast soaked in liquor.' Indeed, drunkenness was an accepted aspect of the Belfast street, along with bookmakers' touts, pawn shops and prostitution. Wife-beating was a common occurrence, yet only as a last resort would the wife take her husband to court. One such court case concerned a labourer charged with continuous neglect of his children. At the hearing his wife declared that he was seldom sober and spent his earnings on drink. On the night in question he struck her several times and then lifted a chair and struck his daughter who was subject to epileptic fits. He was sentenced to two months' hard labour.

At the very bottom of the social scale were the families whose very survival depended on the earnings of wives and children and naturally it was to the linen mills and factories that these women turned to bolster the family income. Wages were not keeping pace with prices with the result that tea, white bread, sugar and condensed milk became the staple diet of the Belfast working class. This, coupled with inadequate housing, an extremely long working day and poor sanitary conditions, led to outbreaks of typhoid fever, consumption and a high infant mortality rate. But among the working class there existed a great community spirit and so it was to their own friends and neighbours that the poor turned when illness or unemployment upset the family budget. Charity, distributed mainly by the clergy, was regarded as demeaning and no self-respecting woman would accept it, while state charity with its stigma of pauperism was to be avoided at all costs. The dread of the workhouse hung over the poor and families would live in utter squalor and penury rather than go 'up the Lisburn Road' [i.e. to the Belfast workhouse].

Belfast, however, was divided not only by economics but by religion and politics. Unionists were suspicious that a growing Irish Nationalism would undermine Belfast's prosperity and the whole country was split by the Home Rule question. Sectarian animosity flourished and rioting became endemic. This was, perhaps, not the best atmosphere to foster Trade

Unionism. Suspicion and fear divided the workforce in their fight for rights, better pay and conditions.

Yet Belfast was not all drab poverty. Naturally not everyone could afford a weekly trip to the Alhambra or Opera House, but most people could look forward to the occasional charabanc trip to Glengormley or Bangor. Then there were also Sunday nights when thousands of people would put on their best clothes and go down to the Custom House steps. Some came to hear the Salvation Army band or the choir or the testimonies of the saved. Young girls came to eye the men; others came for the craic or merely to be seen. Flower-sellers, stick-hawkers, whelk stalls all added to the excitement and colour.

Linen Production

Una Walker

Linen is a fabric woven from the fibres found in the stem of the flax plant. Flax fibres have been used by man since the Stone Age and linen cloth since at least 4,000BC. There were linen-weaving factories in ancient Egypt, staffed by slaves, which produced large quantities of fabric for clothing and embalming. Early accounts of exports from Ireland mention linen, as do descriptions of the dress of the native Irish. In fact the Irish used so much linen—according to one report thirty or forty yards in an individual shirt—that a law was passed in 1537 restricting the quantity of linen to no more than seven yards per shirt. In the seventeenth century linen production was encouraged in Ireland as it offered no opposition to existing industry in England. This was successful; Ireland's woollen trade had been destroyed by the imposition of high export duties and looms were soon converted to weave linen.

By the mid-nineteenth century the manufacture of linen had ceased to be a cottage industry in which individuals worked in their own homes. Thanks to the rapid developments then taking place in technology and science, the industry had undergone a revolution. By 1911 the social and technological changes were complete. In Belfast, mill and factory workers lived in the rows of red-brick houses near their places of work. In rural areas workers walked from their homes to the mill or factory where production was centralised. In 1912 there were 37,292 power looms in Ireland weaving yarn from hundreds of thousands of spindles.

At the beginning of the twentieth century much of the flax for Northern Ireland's linen industry was still home produced. It is a greedy crop which leaves the soil impoverished but it paid the farmer well. Imported seed was sown in March or April and was ready for harvesting in July or August. In order to obtain the longest possible fibres, the flax had to be pulled by hand—an unpleasant job as the strong stems cut into the hand, drawing blood. The flax was tied in bundles and put into a lint dam to ret or rot the hard woody outer casing of the fibres. After ten days the retted flax was removed from the dam, which by then was stinking from the smell of decaying vegetable matter, and left to dry. From there it went to the scutching mill where the dry and flaking woody portions of the stems were removed. At this stage the flax was bought by the spinning mill and the process of transforming vegetable fibres into linen began.

The flax was hand-carded and combed by 'roughers'; it was then machine-carded until it was very fine by 'hacklers'; then it was laid out on spreading boards and drawn out at least four times until long, narrow slivers or ribbons of flax had been produced. The sliver was passed through a roving frame where the flax was drawn out further, received its first twist and was wound onto rove bobbins. The rove bobbins were sent to be wet spun and as many as 120 were set up on each spinning frame. Here the rove passed through a trough of hot water to loosen the gummy substance which holds the fibres together and allowed the yarn, as it made its way through a series of rollers, to be drawn out more and more finely. It was then twisted by a flyer and wound onto the yarn bobbin.

Wet spinners stood between two machines and tended one side of each. When the yarn bobbins were full the machine was stopped, the full bobbins were 'doffed' and then replaced by empty ones. The spinners had to thread the yarn through the eye of the flyer, which was screwed onto the top of each yarn bobbin, and then have the machine working again as soon as possible. If the yarn broke on the way to any of the bobbins, the spinner had to stop that particular flyer and join the broken pieces together; this was known as 'laying up your ends'.

Spun yarn was reeled into hanks and dried; it was then ready to go to the factory to be woven into fabric. Power looms turned out linen, from the very finest cambric for underwear, to strong coarse material for army tents. Complicated jacquard looms produced damask for tablecloths and napkins. No matter what the eventual use of the fabric, most of it came off the loom in the natural brown colour of the flax. Linen was bleached white both by using chemicals and by exposing it to the sun's rays on bleaching greens. Damask was finished in the beetling mill where it was pounded repeatedly until the shiny surface was achieved.

In the early twentieth century there were only four textiles: wool, silk, cotton and linen. Linen, which is strong and long-lasting, was put to many uses. Mail bags were (and still are) made of linen. So were underwear, handkerchiefs, shirts and suits. Because it is very absorbent, it was used in the kitchen and the bathroom. Linen tablecloths and bed-sheets have retained their reputation to this day as being the very best available. Of course some linen was put to humbler uses: empty flour bags were bought by spinners and weavers and made into aprons. Nor should we forget that brown linen was the material upon which scenery was painted for theatres.

Personal Perspectives

'People who could spake for you'

Marie Jones

Growing up in Belfast, from a family whose bread and butter had been the linen mills, the shipyard and the rope works, I had heard the names of Sadie Patterson, Big Jim Larkin, wee Joe Beattie and David Bleakley.

They were not called 'working class heroes' then or 'champions of the cause'; they were known simply as 'People who could spake for you'. We just assumed if we sang about them in skipping rhymes, they must be famous and if they were revered by our Mas and Das, then, without question, they would be revered by us.

So here I was, almost a quarter of a century later along with the rest of the newly-formed Charabanc Theatre Company about to meet Sadie Patterson, union activist, mill-worker, a woman before her time—an extraordinary, ordinary woman. But more importantly, to the mill-workers of Belfast she was one of those rare 'People who could spake for you'.

As we all squeezed into Sadie's small two-up, two-down house in the Woodvale area of Belfast, we got a sense that this would, without doubt, be an extraordinary, ordinary experience.

Everything about that small room felt welcoming, comforting, ordinary and extraordinary. Although spotlessly clean, it was clear that nothing had changed in decades, that the past was important, should be valued and not forgotten. The flowered walls were covered with Sunday-school prize pictures; sepia photographs of men and women in uniform lined the mantelpiece and in the corner stood a glass china cabinet packed with china ornaments with sayings: 'A present from Groomsport/Bangor/Portrush', treasured memories of 'charabanc' trips to the seaside.

This woman who lost her mother early in her teens, who started work in the mills when she was 12, had an aura about her which defied her unpretentious surroundings, but to this day it is still hard to explain. All I can say is, 'you needed to be there'. There she was, now in her late seventies, upright in her chair, composed, almost regal, yet ordinary. It was incredible to think that this simple woman sat face to face and challenged men in power—politicians, mill owners, men who tried to talk her down, make her feel irrelevant. These men no doubt soon realised that they were dealing with a woman with a rare inner strength and an unshakeable belief. They would never have reckoned, when this small unimposing woman walked into their offices, that she was one of those 'People who could spake for you'.

We sat round her like wide-eyed children and listened as she told us about her life and her struggle to fight for the rights of the impoverished mill-workers of Belfast. At one stage she started to tell us, in a matter-of-fact way, 'My mother was a suffragette, you know.' This was incredible; there were shocked and amazed looks all round; we thought working women from Belfast wouldn't know or care about the suffragette movement; it happened in England and the women were mostly middle class. 'But,' she pointed out, 'my mother was a woman before her time. She always told me, if you know of an injustice and do nothing about it, you're as bad as the perpetrator.' She then nodded over to an armchair in the corner and said, 'My mother invited Nye Bevan over to Belfast and he sat there.' We all spoke at once (as was our wont in those days), 'What!!? Nye Bevan? That chair there? Honest to God?!'

Nye Bevan at that time was a British Labour Member of Parliament, had been a leader of the General Strike in 1926, and yet this unheard of mill-worker from Belfast had managed to persuade him to come all the way from London to a small terrace house in the Woodvale. 'Well,' says Sadie, (as if it was the done thing to do), 'my mother knew that Nye Bevan would understand. He had suffered injustices down the mines. She knew if she could get him here, he would be "Somebody who could speak for us".'

It struck most of us that night that we were being party to a history that had never been recorded or written down. Sadie herself had been left an unwritten legacy by her mother, a responsibility which she took on with grace and great courage for the most of her life. It was an unforgettable night. We hung on her every word; she was never angry or self-congratulatory when she recounted her story. She said simply, 'I did what I did, because it was the only right thing to do.' She looked at us; she took us all in and said something I will never forget: 'This story must be told and it's up to you girls to tell it.'

What she was telling us was, I believe, our inspiration for what was to come. She wasn't asking us to have showdowns with mill-owners or challenge politicians. She knew we had an opportunity to use a different kind of power. She was simply telling us that by our words, our drama, we could become 'People who could spake for you'.

Charabanc—a feminist theatre company?

Ian McElhinney

Charabanc was often referred to in the press as a 'feminist' theatre company, even an 'agitprop' company. True, the company was made up of women, but when they started out they were far from storming the barricades. They were young(ish), energetic, but the roles for actresses of that age in the theatre were few and far between. So what did these 'feminists' do? They turned to a couple of men. Firstly to Martin Lynch—a newly-established popular playwright. Could he write them a play, tailored to their needs? Martin, wisely, said no. He suggested rather that they should write it themselves and added, graciously, that he would help. Thus began a collaborative venture with Martin as the 'lynch-pin'. I well remember weekly sessions, usually on a Sunday evening in our front room (in Ravenhill Park) where ideas, characters and storylines were thrashed out.

None of the women was a playwright then. Martin suggested they write from their own experience. So they decided to research their family histories, talk to people—

women mostly (as they would be playing them)—about their working lives, their local communities, their 'hopes, fears and dreams'. This phrase was like a mantra at the time, a working agenda. So the recognised Charabanc style of play-making, based on comprehensive local research and face-to-face interviews, was born. Though others of the group did submit scenes, with time and the editorial rigour of Martin and the director, Marie Jones emerged as the principal writer. As she herself has said elsewhere: it was as if they were all sitting on a charabanc and the driver hadn't turned up; so before she knew it, she filled in. So many of their families had a connection with the linen mills (as, in fact, did so many families throughout the North) that the life of women in the mills became the subject for the first play. So *Lay Up Your Ends* began.

The second man to whom they turned was me, Ian McElhinney, not as a director but as a producer. I was reasonably well-known locally as an actor but I had no obvious credentials for this undertaking and no past experience. However, at that stage I was going out with Marie Jones, so I didn't have much room for negotiation! I think the fact that some of us shared a house in which I took responsibility for working out everyone's bills and utilities persuaded them that I'd be tight with the purse strings and good with money.

Now it was time for me to turn to a number of men. This was largely because the people controlling the purse strings in those days seemed to be men. There were two in particular who were important for us: Alex Clarke and Paddy Devlin. Alex Clarke was the area secretary for Equity (the actors' union). He was a staunch socialist, a warm paternal man, who believed the union should produce results and not just trumpet good intentions. He ensured an introduction for us to the ACE scheme run then by the Department of Economic

Development. Under this scheme a percentage of salaries would be underwritten if we could find the remaining percentage from other sources and if the appropriate conditions pertained. Together we made sure they did.

Paddy Devlin was possibly the only serious supporter of the theatre on Belfast City Council at the time. He was a fierce and passionate fighter for anything he believed in. He once famously told another councillor that he wouldn't recognise a point of order if it fell from the ceiling and hit him on the head! To Paddy we were all 'mates'—girls and all. He helped me pressurise the Council into giving us a significant amount of funding from (Belfast City Council) Leisure Services in return for our playing in a number of their centres. This gave us our percentage to balance the money from the Department of Economic Development and we were up and running.

Our front room became the office by day and the think-tank by night. Marie started writing with Martin; Brenda Winter started working with me. I remember insisting that Brenda produce receipts and account for every item of petty cash. The only time I ever asked her to do anything where I had a reasonable conviction that she would comply! A few years later the tables were turned when I was directing a show which she was producing and I had to fight tooth and nail for every penny. It was a tough school and we were learning on the hoof. Budgets were tight; not everyone was supportive; in fact some were obstructive. Some were even condescending, perhaps unwittingly, to this 'women's group' even if they were helping us. Ultimately they were fearful because of the extraordinary success of this first production and the realisation that Charabanc was going to be around for a long time to come.

So the women moved in and ultimately the men became

redundant (as they do!). This was not a revolution, just a natural progression. In its prime Charabanc did have female actors, female directors, a female administrator, female designers and female stage management. However, the issues pursued were always universal, rather than gender-specific. Nobody needed to 'beat a big drum'. The integrity of the people always shone through and so too the integrity of the work.

The Russian Tour

Martin Lynch

My experiences in the early days of Charabanc Theatre Company were ones I look back at with great fondness. We had many great times. The five original actresses, Marie Jones, Eleanor Methven, Carol Moore, Brenda Winter and Maureen Macauley, director Pam Brighton, Board members Ian McElhinney and Cherrie McIlwaine, all added up to a truly dynamic operation that I believe has made a significant contribution to the history of Belfast and, indeed, Irish theatre. But there is one episode in that history that still has me struggling to determine whether it was a significant contribution or a major blemish ...

Ian McElhinney rang me one Saturday night and announced the great news that Charabanc Theatre Company had been invited to perform a play I had co-written with the Company, *Lay Up Your Ends*, on a tour of three cities in the former Soviet Union. Ian wanted to know if I could attend a meeting to discuss this offer as there were quite a lot of things to be considered. So, for the first time since I was nine, I missed *Match of the Day* on a Saturday night and headed over to a house on Ravenhill Park where two or three of the Charabanc members lived and where all the meetings usually took place. (There's a book to be written about the goings-on in that house that would chronicle modern Northern Irish theatre history as much as, say, a history of the Lyric Theatre, but that's for another day). After about three hours and approximately another seven meetings, Charabanc finally agreed to take up the offer of a tour of the Soviet Union. As I remember it, the deal was that we were to travel to the Soviet Union on a chartered flight organised by the British-Soviet Friendship Society and a fellow called John Russell. Charabanc's part of the deal was that it had to gather up a certain number of travellers beyond the members of the Company to help make up the cost of hiring the plane.

Hence, in the year of 1984, we headed off on what became known as 'The Russian Tour' and what I now consider one of the most memorable trips of my life. Included on the trip was a motley collection of friends, media types, thespians, relatives, hangers-on, complete strangers and probably a few stowaways for all I knew. As well as the members of the Company, names I remember include: Kate Smith, Jeannie Johnston, Joanne Woods and John O'Hara of UTV, Louis Edmonson and Judith Elliott of the BBC, Eugene Maloney (the *Irish News*), Harry Donaghy of Lower Falls and Anne Corr from Derry City. Ironically, Ian McEhinney couldn't make it due to work commitments.

The notion of visiting the Soviet Union to me was hugely intriguing. Having read and studied so much about its people and its history, I was now going to be able to see at first hand what it was really like. The first shock was at the airport when

I presented my passport and had my face studied by a nineteen-year-old uniformed official for approximately seven minutes. I'm not joking. Unrelenting, unsmiling, cemented staring for seven minutes. We did get the diplomatic treatment in that we didn't have to check our bags through but instead were whisked straight on to a waiting luxury bus. On the bus I looked around for the rest of the Charabanc actors but it was then that we discovered that some 'Charabancers' were 'more equal than others'. It turned out that the five actresses, director Pam Brighton, stage crew Paul Myler and Stephen McManus and administrator Janet Mackle had been separated into an élite group who were to be ferried around by limousine, accommodated in a four-star hotel and generally given special status for the entire trip. This caused 'outrage' among the remaining 25 travellers. We retired to the pub in the hotel and had a union meeting. Very soon we were smiling and joking. We worked out that the 'special' group—which was hastily dubbed the A-Team—would be stuck with all the official protocol rubbish that would inevitably be an important part of this trip. As well as having the burden of having to perform the play a number of times, they could look forward to endless official receptions, meetings and tiresome 'what is the Northern Ireland Troubles about' explanations with Mayors, Cultural attachés, politicians, reporters, KGB spies etc. whilst we could ... carouse. Carouse and generally cause consternation and turmoil in the well-ordered everyday life of the Soviet Union. The A-Team could shove their special status!!

The B-Team, as we were now known, was allocated an interpreter/guide called Irina. She was brilliant but inevitably had great difficulties with us. For the first four days she traipsed us from museum to museum, important historic building to important historic building. At the end of the fourth day there was a rebellion. Not quite on the scale of 1917 but every bit as resolute.

'Irina, you don't need to call for us tomorrow morning.'

'Excuse me? But I must call for you. I am your appointed interpreter and tomorrow at 8 a.m. we are due to visit the important ... '

'Irina, your historic buildings are terrific but we've had enough, we're tired.'

'Oh, but you must be in the hotel lobby by 7.45 a.m. The Cultural Attaché in charge of your trip is coming to ... '

'Irina, we've had enough!!'

I was sick of the constant official guidance. I was in the great city of Moscow. I wanted to meet ordinary Russian people in their own environment without any interference. Conscious of the George Bernard Shaw quote after he visited the nascent Soviet Union in 1926: 'I have seen the future and it works', I wanted to see as much as I could of how the Soviet Union worked for ordinary people. We met in the hotel pub and I asked for volunteers for an independent exploration of Moscow the next day. I got about ten hands. Game on.

The next morning the Bolshevik Ten including myself, Eugene Maloney, big Harry Donaghy, Michael McCloskey, Anne Corr, Gerry 'Somebody' from Limerick etc. refused all banging on doors, telephone calls, threats, and waited until the official party, led by Irina and the Cultural Attaché, had left the hotel to spend a fifth day staring at another collection of buildings. (I have all the photos of the first four days and they are fantastic but ...). My idea was that we would simply get on the underground, travel as far as the train would go, then get off and go and explore. An indication of how the day was going to turn out was the sight of ten Northern Irish people conversing   with   various   Moscovites   about   the unpronounceable names on the train map and where we should get off and not a word of understanding among the lot of us. The Moscow tube, of course, is famous the world over for its beautiful stations (some were like small palaces) and schedule promptness.

We got off at the end of the line and emerged from the underground. I found myself standing in ... Andersonstown. At least, that's what it reminded me of. A slightly run-down version of Andersonstown but essentially it was a huge, sprawling public authority housing estate. The next step was to get into somebody's house and talk to them. For a moment I became the Bolshevik One as the others recoiled at this notion. I managed to convince them that we could do it. I led the group into a block of flats (apartments, if you're American or live in South Belfast) and knocked on a ground floor door. After a long wait the door opened and a woman peeked out from behind the door. Ten people stared back at her. I got the impression she wasn't properly dressed. The next part is madness. I went into my broken-English spiel.

'Hello. We ... (I point at the others) ... are from Irelande ... we would like to come in ... (point in at her hallway) ... and talk ... (make a closing and unclosing motion with my hand up at my mouth) ... to you ... ' (I point at her).

Bang! The door is slammed quickly.

'C'mon Martin, this is crazy; let's go.'

'No, no, hold on, hold on, we'll try a few more doors. The Soviet Union has created a new system of living from the rest of the world since 1917,' I point out, 'so we're here and I'm not leaving until we check it out.'

We walked up a flight of stairs and I knocked another door. Absolutely no reply. I knocked another. Same. Brushing aside more group apprehensions, I led them up another flight. I knocked on another door. This time, after a few minutes, a man appears. He is in his late sixties, bald, checked shirt, cardigan and corduroy trousers and in his slippers. He immediately smiles. I start my spiel. Remember, as he looks at me, he is looking at ten strange faces staring back at him.

'Hello. We ... (pointing at the others) ... would like ... '

He understood exactly what I was saying and immediately, and enthusiastically, invited us into his flat with a sweep of his hands. The flat reminded me of my grandmother's flat back home on the New Lodge Road. Small, neat and comfortable but with 1950s furniture. The TV was on and it's always strange how you can tell these things, but he was obviously watching the Russian version of *Coronation Street*. Same sets, same actors, same dramatics. In a language he didn't understand a word of, we asked him what the programme was. He told us what it was in a language we didn't understand a word of. We all—him too—nodded in exact understanding. Yes, *Coronation Street*. I looked at the walls. One wall was covered in framed photos of family members and Soviet Communist Party emblems. I pointed to a woman whom I reckoned was his wife and asked who she was. Animated, he closed his two hands flat together and placed them against his leaning head. He then made a couple of sharp, thrusting movements crossing his open flat hands across each other in front of him. Then he pointed at his wedding finger. Interpretation? It was his wife and she was dead, gone, kaput. I pointed at some photos of young men and women. He immediately held out his open flat hand down at knee height. These were his children. Then he shrugged and made a sweeping motion with his hands towards the door. They were all gone and living elsewhere now. He was now alone. I pointed at the Soviet emblems. He smiled, made a clenched fist with his right hand and held it up in the air. He was a Communist Party member. He went to a drawer and showed us his membership card. All this without a single common word among us.

The ten of us then stood in the middle of this man's small living room, looking around, nodding and searching for something else to say. Eventually, we decided to go. He walked us to the door. At the door Eugene Maloney whispered to me that we should give the man some money as a gift for allowing us to visit inside his home. Eugene and I quickly put together ten pounds sterling and I held it out to him smiling. His hand went up—like a points peeler—immediately. He continued to smile but he made it clear he didn't want any money. On the spur of the moment Eugene pulled a packet of Wrigley's Spearmint chewing gum out of his top pocket and offered it. The man happily received it. We said our goodbyes in English and he in Russian and we parted.

Lay Up Your Ends was performed in Moscow and was well received by an invited audience of the great and the good. In Leningrad (St Petersburg), the play was performed again and this time a couple of hundred students of English were invited as part of the audience. The idea was that attendance at the play would help improve their English! The poor souls. Unfortunately for them, *Lay Up Your Ends* is a large tract of 'Belfastese' and delivered, of course, without concession to man nor beast. By the end of the performance, I think I saw more bewildered student faces in one room than I'd ever seen before.

In Leningrad, because it was billed as a tour of the battle sites of the October Revolution 1917, we happily rejoined Irina and her band of bored sightseers. Things were going well until Irina began to point out certain buildings, barricades and street corners near the Winter Palace where, she was sure, all the main action took place. Harry Donaghy, fanatical Russian history student, piped up: 'Sorry love, you're wrong there.'

'Pardon.'

'The first batch of workers weren't stopped at Samonersky Bridge; they were stopped at Nikolayersky Bridge. Over there.'

Our entire party turned and looked in the opposite direction.

Harry, who had never been in Russia in his life at this point, (he later returned and married a Russian woman and they now live happily in West Belfast) pointed to the Nikolayersky Bridge. From then on, whilst I do not suggest that Harry actually took over as guide, he went on to do most of the talking in and around the Winter Palace while Irina listened like the rest of us. Irina really had a hard time with us.

In the meantime, apart from us all being together at the play performances, we seldom saw the A-Team of Messrs Jones, Brighton etc. Once or twice their limousine passed near our bus and we exchanged fusillades of verbal abuse and the odd rotten tomato. I did learn from exasperated A-Teamer, Paul Myler, that on one occasion whilst the B-Team went off and found a great restaurant/bar and had a great night mixing with the locals, the A-Team had attended a reception with tea where they heard a two-hour speech about the proposed five-year plan for Soviet agriculture on the Uzbekistan Steppes.

The journey from Moscow to St Petersburg provided me with my first ever overnight train journey. It was everything you might imagine: romantic, olde-worlde and filled with great craic. After dinner on the train—the A-Team was, for once, forced to live among us—we all congregated in the diner/bar carriage for drinks. Within hours the Northern Ireland visitors had almost drunk the train dry. First, they ran out of beer, then vodka, then whiskey—it was four in the morning by now—then champagne (cheap as anything)! Eventually, the party took a dip when they stopped serving us. A young uniformed guard was brought in to clear the carriage and get us all to our beds. His orders were immediately drowned out with a chorus of 'Whiskey in the Jar'. He was distracted. This man was used to citizens obeying him. The singing continued but the energy began to decline. Suddenly, the woman in charge of the carriage, who had retired to a seat counting the takings on an abacus, took pity on us. She disappeared and returned with two crates of FREE Russian beer. The party was on again. At around six a.m. the guard returned for about the tenth time. He was getting really angry now and was shouting at us to leave the carriage. Within a few minutes, however, Jeannie Johnston was waltzing with him, Kate Smith was dancing up and down the aisle wearing his Soviet cap and Harry Donaghy was trying on his jacket. (I still have his hat in my house.) The poor guard ended up sitting down and giving us a rendition of the only song he knew in English, 'Yesterday' by the Beatles. He gave up trying to get us to bed.

A great highlight of the trip was when the group was invited to a see a locally written and produced play in Vilnius, Lithuania, one of the then republics in the Soviet Union. It was a terrific example of creative, physical theatre where human bodies and minimal props were used in a way I had never quite seen before to such an extent that, although the play was performed totally in Lithuanian, we understood 95 per cent of what was going on.

On our last night of the trip in Leningrad, we decided to organise an Irish ceili for ourselves and all the Russian people, guides, escorts, interpreters, we had come to know. Having bluffed my way through many a ceili night in my youth, I took it on myself to shout and manhandle a really motley crew of Leningrad civic dignitaries, Russian waiters, South Derry Protestants, English college lecturers and plain footless actors, through a repertoire of ceili dances. The Waves of Tory looked more like the Battle of the Bogside.

Knowing we had a flight home at some ungodly hour, I got to bed at about three a.m. When the alarm woke me next morning, I packed and made my way out to the hotel corridor and the lift. Before the lift arrived I thought I could hear singing. As my lift got closer, the singing got closer. The doors opened and there was big Harry Donaghy and his new-found best mate, Gerry 'Somebody' from Limerick, with their arms wrapped round each other—bottle of Russian vodka in hand—and murdering their version of 'Raglan Road'. They hadn't been to bed yet but had at least the good sense to be heading for the airport along with the rest of us.

'How's it goin', lads?' I said.

'Martin,' big Harry replied enthusiastically 'y'wanna taste this vodka. It's heavy duty. It's so heavy duty it makes your hair sore ..."that her dark hair would weave a snare, that I might one day rue" ... '

Yes, my experience with the Charabanc Theatre Company was one that I wouldn't have missed for the world. There were some memorable times. The night I sat in a packed Arts Theatre as the audience gave a standing ovation to *Lay Up Your Ends* was a highlight. In the next two nights we packed out the old Shankill Stadium Centre and the Andersonstown Leisure Centre, reassuring us that our work was relevant to both sides of our community. When we performed the play at the old Brookfield Mill in Ardoyne to a packed house of ex-mill-

orkers, I was particularly proud that some of the people I
d based characters on or had referenced in the action of the
ay were in the audience. These were memorable times. But
mehow, deep down in me, none—none—surpassed the, by
w, legendary Russian tour.

Impulse to Imagination

Carol Moore

It's 2nd November 1982 and, as usual, I am over at Marie ar Eleanor's place. We might have been having dinner or drin but definitely moaning about the lack of work for actresses Belfast—think of Bob Dylan at a low ebb and you're right the with us. But that night changed our lives! Channel Four four its way into our living-rooms. Cutting edge and controversi this new channel was going to attempt everything the riv channels wouldn't or couldn't do.

But Channel Four was in dispute with the advertisers ar high expectations of its launch turned into a damp weekend Glengormley. (Believe me, I grew up there so I know what I' talking about!) Instead, a female revue called The Ravir Beauties was aired, with three English actresses giving tl culturally minded a menu of poems, songs and sketches fro what seemed like a theatre production recreated in a black-b studio setting. Is all of this beginning to sound familiar?

I ushered Marie and Eleanor in from the other roo exclaiming, 'Look at these women! Why can't we d

>mething like this? Why can't we write our own material?' Vell, there's the rub. On the one hand it felt so obvious but vould a lack of confidence at attempting to write our own naterial become the stumbling block?

Fast forward to a year of Sunday-night meetings where the rustration of unemployment fuelled a motley group of .ctresses (Brenda and Maureen were also on board) to examine 00 years of Belfast's history, encouraged and cajoled by our nentor, Martin Lynch. Indeed the mill-girls' strike of 1911 vould catapult us into a period of history and open a door into he lives of working-class women that would impact greatly on he company's theatrical and political ethos from that point >nwards. To be invited to have tea with the iconic trade union activist Miss Sadie Patterson and welcomed into the homes of nany retired mill-girls, like Florrie Banks, Kitty Irwin, Anna Winter and Bella O'Hara, was both an honour and an education.

Bella O'Hara's little house, nestled behind York Street, was adjacent to the beginning of the West Link. Even in the early eighties you were struck by how history sat cheek by jowl with redevelopment. Shawled and sitting on her settle bed by an open fire, Bella held forth on important issues like Queen Victoria's sexual appetite as well as personal accounts of entering the mill as a doffer at the age of 14. But I will always fondly remember Emily Stephenson. Emily lived in a maze of streets off the Shankill Road, like the kitchen houses built all over Belfast to accommodate mill workers. Emily would have been in her late 70s but had a memory as agile as a twenty-year-old. On leaving, she handed me a tin. When I opened it, I found her 'scraper' and 'picker' with the name 'Emily' inscribed on them. These were the essential tools of a mill-girl. 'I won't be needing these. Take them if they are any use to you, daughter.' I continue to treasure them.

These memorable encounters epitomise the heart of *Lay u* *Your Ends*. The play was both agitprop and music hall, roug theatre but with dramatic sophistication. Like The Ravin Beauties on Channel Four that night, five Belfast actresse offered Belfast and beyond a style of theatre that captured bot the imagination and the heart. We threw out the theatrical rule book and wrote a new one. It was called Charabanc.

Charabanc Chronicles

Cherrie McIlwaine

Charabanc Theatre Company was born out of imagination, humour, empathy, determination and a healthy amount of desperation fuelled by the fact that at the time opportunities for jobbing actresses were thin on the ground.

When the company-to-be and a few friends got together at Marie and Ian's house to talk about the possibilities of creating a new company, the ground was set for two vital Charabanc characteristics which were to become even more evident and important as dream became reality.

The first grew from Martin Lynch's advice when he said, in encouraging the girls to create their own work, 'Write about what you know.'

The second was not just to 'talk the talk' but to 'walk the walk' and in the case of *Lay Up Your Ends* that meant to libraries, to the Public Records Office and, crucially, to the women whose lives the play so richly and vividly represents.

Even for those of us on the margins it was a time of infectious and feverish energy. Industry and drive characterised the pursuit of this play from first thoughts and early drafts to a play with a shape and something to say. That said, none of us could have anticipated the way in which the play was received or the impact which it was to have on theatre in Northern Ireland.

First nights are always special—something to do with the release of all that harnessed creative energy and the fact that people have paid good money for tickets and that, ready or not, the curtain must go up.

The first night of *Lay Up Your Ends* was somewhere beyond special. For a start it was a Sunday and the city streets were largely quiet in that restrained Belfast-on-a-Sunday sort of way. Then there was the fact that this was a first night for new company with a brand new play of their own making.

The atmosphere in the theatre as we got ready during the afternoon was tight with excitement.

Finishing touches were being made to the exhibition of beautiful linens for the foyer display, which served both as an introduction to and a retrospective reminder, if one was needed, of the hardship involved in the process of linen manufacture.

Paddy Scanlon and I were front-of-house staff for the night and our box-office duties seemed straightforward enough. But time does funny things when deadlines loom and hours disappeared like minutes as the 'tech' and last minute adjustments took place behind the dark doors of the auditorium.

The pressure was palpable with Pam Brighton's muffled directions morphing through the door to those of us in the foyer. By the second it seemed, there were more and more of us as the audience grew and grew and grew until there was no more room in the foyer and the stream of people threaded its way backwards down the stairs and out into Botanic Avenue.

The Arts Theatre had never seen its like and certainly not on a Sunday night. The box-office was in a state of controlled chaos but the craic was great as everyone waited for the 'go' and the doors opened to allow the audience through.

I can only imagine how the cast must have felt as the curtain went up and more importantly how they felt when it came down again to the kind of applause which every actor, every director and every writer dreams of.

Lay Up Your Ends, to quote from the flyer, invited us all to 'discover the mills, meet the doffin' mistress, face the poverty, shun the workhouse, listen to the great public speakers, frolic on the Custom House steps and relive the lives of the women of 1911'.

And on a Sunday night in the summer of 1983, we did.

The Charabanc had well and truly arrived.

Contemporary Media Coverage

The Lynch Scalpel
Leaves Them in Stitches

Eugene Maloney

As uproariously funny as it is politically poignant, *Lay Up Your Ends* by the newly formed Charabanc Theatre Company relives the lives of a group of women mill workers in the Belfast of 1911.

Yet as the play traces how their dismal working conditions led them first to strike and then to form the Irish Transport and General Workers' Union specially for mill-girls, it never once disintegrates into mere political diatribe. The five-woman cast, backed by a semi-dumb street musician, strike a perfect balance between frequently bawdy comedy and raw social comment, to deliver one of the most powerful works to come out of Belfast for some time.

Lay Up Your Ends is full of vintage Belfast humour and if Karl Marx is to be found in the script, Groucho is not far away. The play is currently being staged in local leisure and community centres but when it opened at Belfast Arts Theatre for a special performance, it was a case of standing room only.

The company, set up to explore dramatically the history of

Belfast both pleasant and unpleasant, has received support both from Action for Community Employment and the City Council.

Author Martin Lynch and the cast achieve the play's aims magnificently. For not only does the plot take us on a guided tour of the Belfast of the pre-Great War years, it also throws up a skilful blend of characters.

There is Belle, played by Marie [Sarah] Jones, who after 30 years in the York St mill, looks to trade unionism and James Connolly for a better future. With a perfect mixture of maternal affection and the razor-sharp wit of the streets, it is she who prompts her workmates to go on strike in the hope of improving conditions.

Eleanor Methven, as country girl Florrie Brown, turns in a sterling performance as a lass, big and direct, who having set her mind on the need for rebellion, never once questions it.

Then there is Carol Moore [Scanlan] full of birdlike tenacity. She plays Ethna McNamara with a typically caustic Belfast outlook towards life, sex and her husband.

Rounding off the quintet of characters, each of them perfectly formed and presented, are Maureen Macauley as young, pretty Mary Rooney who longs for a better future on the stage, and Brenda Winter who, as Lizzie McCormick, is torn between supporting the strike and avoiding what her husband warns is the Papism of Connolly.

The play also throws up a succession of other characters: husbands, mill bosses, even a local ladies' guild, all of them played by the five women. These character changes are achieved frequently by changing accents and with the women donning jackets over their long skirts.

A Belfastman without pretension, Martin Lynch's forte

seems to be laughter and politics. Long may he continue. *Lay Up Your Ends* is definitely not to be missed. A history lesson was never so much fun.

Irish News, 16th May 1983

Impressive Women

Charlie Fitzgerald

An all-women theatre company probably made history in Belfast last night, if only by having the queues stretching from the Arts Theatre the length of Botanic Avenue clamouring for admission.

The play they were waiting to see is a new work, *Lay Up Your Ends*, scripted by five actresses of the new Charabanc Theatre Company with the help of Belfast playwright, Martin Lynch.

It owes its authenticity to a brilliant research job on the Belfast of 1911 based on the mill-girls' strike.

To paraphrase an old theatrical expression: 'All Belfast life of the day is here'—the Alhambra music-hall, the Custom House steps on a Sunday night, the wee bit of brass and the scrubbed steps of the terraced houses, the drudgery, the long slave-wage hours of the workers and above all the horrendous atmosphere of the 'Satanic Mills' that made this city a great industrial power but a slum for most of its inhabitants.

It is a chronicle perhaps more than a drama, but as vividly alive a chronicle as anything Holinshed ever produced for

Shakespeare to base his plays on and it has the reality of our own history. The performances from Marie [Sarah] Jones, Carol Moore [Scanlan], Eleanor Methven, Maureen Macauley and Brenda Winter are just stunning.

It was they who conceived the idea of Charabanc to give themselves work and what they intend in bringing to this historical, theatrical pageant as it moves around Ulster, may prove to be one of the worthiest theatrical ideas of the decade.

It owes much to the now-defunct Playzone concept of which Marie Jones was part and its style of presentation draws much on Martin Lynch's experience of producing colourful historical drama for BBC Radio Ulster.

Belfast News Letter 16th May 1983

Dramatic View of Life in the Mill

Jane Bell

A packed-to-bursting Belfast Civic Arts Theatre was the venue last night for the first excursion of the newly-formed Charabanc Theatre Company.

Every seat was taken with everyone from little kids to grannies on board. The destination was Belfast 1911, the play *Lay Up Your Ends* focusing on the lives of five particular women involved in the York St mill strike of that year.

The script with its rich humour and colourful Belfast language was co-written by Turf Lodge playwright Martin Lynch and the company. Their research included talking to people who had lived through that time and whose experiences shaped the play.

Many threads are drawn together to give the piece its texture. The harsh oppressive clamour of the mill contrasts with the buzz of excitement at the Custom House steps, a favourite Sunday night meeting place of the time with its hawkers and soap-box preachers.

There's the haunting black figure of the money-lender and a

sharp portrait of a life of ease and trivia in the mill-owner's lady's drawing-room.

Trade Unionism, class issues, poverty and sectarian animosity are all major themes in this play directed by Pam Brighton.

Belfast born-and-bred humour is rife in the play and was much enjoyed. Mostly it was used to best effect but, now and again, it drowned the poignancy of a particular moment. Humour is a sharp and probing dramatic tool and overuse can blunt its edge.

There were some excellent performances from the actresses at the heart of the production. Their 'take-offs' of the male figures in the story were dead on.

Marie [Sarah] Jones gave a strong performance as the motivating Belle Thompson and Carol Moore [Scanlan] skilfully handled her role as the tormented Ethna McNamara.

The cast and playwright had a well-deserved standing ovation at the close of the show.

The play—at the Arts last night for one night only—is to tour community and leisure centres. Long may the Charabanc roll.

Belfast Telegraph, 16th May 1983

Nothing Run of the Mill

Paul Hadfield

Opening in the Arts Theatre on 15th May, and then going on to tour community and leisure centres, theatres and festivals in the province (and possibly to tour textile centres in England) is a new play on the workers in the linen mills in Belfast at the turn of the century. This is the collective achievement of the members of the Charabanc Theatre Company formed by five women actors: Marie Jones; Eleanor Methven; Carol Moore; Brenda Winter and Maureen Macauley, with Dai Jenkins as composer/musician and Martin Lynch as script co-ordinator.

Rather than accept 'resting', these actors decided to create work—to research, write, perform, sell and tour their own show and, with Ian McElhinney as activist and fund-raiser, the project was born. They have opened up contact with many of the women who, at the Custom House steps, first heard James Connolly describe them as the 'linen slaves of Belfast'. They have been advised by Sadie Patterson, mesmerised by Bella O'Hara, lent valuable historical documents on the linen workers' strike by Paddy Devlin, are being directed by Pam Brighton from the Hull Truck Theatre Company and financed by the ACE scheme, the Belfast City Council and the Arts Council.

Theatre collectives are not new. Over the past two decades, particularly in the United States, they have revitalised the traditional and often formulaic connections between script and performance in ways that have been innovative, organic and interesting. Integral to this revitalisation is a fresh examination of what a script is, what it does, where it comes from and what it means if it ever makes it to performance.

This sense of dramatic form can only be acquired through practice and Martin Lynch's value to the project seems less to have been what he has written than in the questions he has posed about what audiences ultimately can take. This simple dictum is the filter through which a range of disparate material has had to pass before rehearsals could begin: interviews; old press cuttings; union records; books; reminiscences; personal experiences. It is always painful to see something that excited you when you discovered it being subsequently discarded; yet the willingness of individuals to allow this to happen generates a unique sense of significance in democratic principles.

Talking to Charabanc one cannot help being affected by their commitment both to each other and to the job. What is important is their determination to make the project work theatrically—a point which similar groups often overlook in the inevitable euphoria of collective creativity.

This awareness of the end product has also honed their sense of their audience. Conventional theatrical performances often sublimate this sense to the mechanics of theatre, to recognised patterns of attendance in any given theatre space. Leisure centre audiences know and expect little or nothing from the conventional theatre. Working in these contexts is fraught with risk but the rewards can be greater. Working in non-theatre spaces is ultimately vital because largely class-orientated theatre practice does not reflect the changing structures of society in the way that collective and community-based projects do.

The spin-off from such a project is considerable. In personal terms, those involved have grown in both confidence and competence by confronting a range of skills entirely new to them—research, interviewing, writing, organisation, publicity, fund-raising. In social terms, the community benefits from the whole recycling process of taking people's life experience, rendering it in art and giving it back to them, set in a wider context. And the world of theatre here is invigorated by the energy, reach and scale of the project, by the wider competence and new skills gained by the local members of the theatre community who form the company, by new audiences for theatre who are touched by such work and by the commitment to accessible but serious forms of theatre.

This, finally, is the sort of work we must be proud and quick to encourage. There is nothing run of the mill about it.

Fortnight, May 1983

The Past Put Through the Mill

Rosalind Carne

Belfast audiences on both sides of the sectarian divide are packing the city's community centres to see *Lay Up Your Ends*, a fast, broadly comic and politically biting play about the 1911 strike in the linen mills.

The company involved, Charabanc, was created at the beginning of this year by five actresses, tired of the relentless cycle of unemployment and uninspiring female roles. Committed to producing work that reflected the lives of local women, they researched, improvised and eventually produced a script in collaboration with playwright Martin Lynch, who was resident writer at the Lyric from 1980-82. In April this year they invited the English director Pam Brighton to join them and the resulting show opened at the Arts Theatre on 15th May.

Since then they have created their own touring circuit, stretching from the heart of Provo territory to the bastions of Ulster Unionism. I caught up with them on their recent return visit to the Arts and two days later amidst a throng of former mill-hands in the Beltext Community Centre, a shabby room in a disused mill in Catholic Ardoyne. Response was enthusiastic on both occasions but there was a big difference between the laughter of appreciation in the first place and the excitement of recognition in the second.

The audience in the Ardoyne roared with approval at the authentic, deafening sound of the spinning room, the original black shawls, the details of the craft, its tools and jargon, the crude language. They joined in the songs, exchanging reminiscences as the play progressed. But there was a concentrated silence at the moments of emotional intensity, moments that take the piece a step beyond a mere hymn to working-class bravado, however realistic, and on to something both psychologically intricate and dramatically rewarding.

A large screen forms the backcloth, demonstrating the progression from flax to finished garment, a neat visual suggestion of the labour theory of value. Popping in and out from behind, the five actresses play a host of parts, male and female, often simply by changing position, altering the tilt of a shawl or putting on a cloth cap. Original songs give the flavour of the period, a time when most people hovered around the breadline.

The company includes Catholics and Protestants and though there is nothing exceptional in this in middle-class theatrical circles, it is significant in the light of their commitment to concentrating on issues which override the usual antagonisms of the north. And they quickly discovered how much people love to laugh at themselves—Charlie, the bigoted Protestant, gets the best reception on his home ground, Shankill.

The crucial thing for me, coming from the faintly dispirited atmosphere of London, was not the show itself, but the feeling that this marked the beginning of an alternative theatre movement in a place which has relied for a long time on the inspiration of outsiders. There have been important new writers in recent years, among whom Lynch is probably the best known locally, but never has there been such an extensive and successful tour of the estates.

'People are glad to see a play about women and the mills and not about sectarianism,' said Brenda Winter, who plays the nervous Lizzie, unwilling to risk her precarious social and domestic standing by joining the strike. 'So many things have happened in Belfast—they are crying out to have plays written about them.'

Much of the research consisted of taped interviews with women who had worked in the mills in the 1930s. The industry died out a few years ago, but it used to dominate the city and the subject was guaranteed a vast, receptive audience. It will be hard to produce an equally powerful successor but the company is determined to continue to draw on Belfast's hidden oral history, as well as to maintain their fruitful collaboration with Martin Lynch.

Lynch was born and still lives in Turf Lodge, a working-class Catholic district of West Belfast, and his primary commitment is not artistic but political. A member of the Workers' Party, the successor to the Official wing of the Republican movement, he turned playwright overnight in 1974 when John Arden and Margaretta D'Arcy's *Non-Stop Connolly Show* arrived on his estate. Suddenly it became clear that the stage could be an effective rostrum and though he is well aware of the dangers of ideological battering, he has never lost his conviction that the playwright's concerns are more public than private. 'I'm not going to change my style to play to a minority,' he told me. Collaborating with five women has been surprisingly harmonious. Two of them, Marie Jones and

Carol Moore, wrote sizeable portions of the dialogue themselves and Lynch is unusually unpossessive about his work. He is perfectly happy to let them drop a scene, re-write or add a passage while he is not there. Pam Brighton insisted on extensive pruning when she arrived and there have been continual alterations and additions during the run.

Lay Up Your Ends tours Belfast until mid-July, when it stops for a two-week run at the Group Theatre. There are plans for a tour of the south in August and hopes of a trip to England in September. In spite of the unfamiliarity of the material and much of the language, the play and particularly performances should be strong enough to withstand the journey and I would welcome the chance of another view of an all-women's show that exudes some of the humour and exuberance we seem to have lost over here.

Stage Guardian, 8th July 1983

Lay Up Your Ends at the John Player

Gerry Colgan

During the interval, a plummy voice behind me assured its female companion that what we were watching was propagandist, might entertain the workers from Dunlop's, but was definitely, quite definitely, not art. An inexplicable inarticulacy prevented me from advising its owner to go boil his fat head, thus putting it to some useful function. The result should be a supply of rich mutton soup sufficient to serve the Simon Community for at least a week.

This production by Belfast's Charabanc Company is the result of a workshop collaboration between playwright Martin Lynch and the five superb actresses who enact it. It centres on the strike in 1911 of Belfast's women mill-workers and around it develops a panorama of human misery and dignity, of despair redeemed by laughter and courage.

I know that Henry Ford said history is bunk, and I consider him an idiot. Or maybe he just read the wrong historians. This play is history and it is part of that truth that makes us whole. Fires were lit in those days that today burn undimmed and a live evocation of this quality and conviction transmits the warmth across the footlights to enfold and enthrall its audience.

From the moment that the crashing noise of the mill beats upon our ears, we are captive. The suffering that prevails over fear and sends the strikers to the streets is vividly portrayed. Hostile husbands, predatory money-lenders, the privation of real hunger and the conflict generated in women watching their children suffer; all are relived. And so are the crudities, the drinking, the wrangling, inevitable under such stress.

No praise could be excessive for the five performances that recreate such diversity and richness of human experience. Marie Jones, Carol Moore, Eleanor Methven, Brenda Winter and Maureen Macauley, they are superb. Pam Brighton directs without a discernible flaw and Una Walker's costume and set design are totally in tune. It is, I suppose, the luck of the festival draw that the play was allotted only four performances. It would be inexplicable if any of them played to less than full houses.

Irish Times, 7th October, 1983
as part of the paper's coverage
of the Dublin Theatre Festival

Theatre from the Mills

Fionnuala O'Connor

With a line of chairs and a black shawl apiece, the five actresses in Charabanc become mill-girls on an outing in Belfast in 1911, trying to keep their spirits up in the middle of a doomed strike. In Belfast (1983) they took their Charabanc for ten weeks round the city's community centres and met warmth and nostalgia.

In Ardoyne, in a former mill, a roomful of old mill-workers watched them perform. In Ligoniel a man helper brought on the shawls and there was a buzz of reminiscence: 'Ah, look at that, do you remember ... ?'

The tour of Belfast was a deliberate attempt to show the play, *Lay Up Your Ends*, (the command to stop for re-tying when yarn broke between two machines) to the community it came from in a less formal setting than a theatre proper. The actresses spent several months researching, most of it among former mill-girls, and were determined that they should see the result.

Shared Experience

Marie Jones, Brenda Winter, Eleanor Methven, Maureen Macauley and Carol Moore have a variety of theatrical experience among them and a shared experience of unemployment in Belfast. They came together in January determined in Brenda's words 'to write something for ourselves with challenging parts because when we actually got work, the parts weren't very interesting. Initially we thought of a revue or play already written—then we met Martin Lynch and asked him to write us a play about women in Belfast and he said, "Nonsense. Write it yourselves".' They compromised and wrote it as a joint enterprise.

They had all been unemployed for long periods, some longer than others, a situation not unconnected with production policy in Belfast theatres. 'The Lyric has a policy of bringing in people from England—that's healthy enough. Keeps people from becoming insular, but it's hit our age group (mid-twenties to mid-thirties) of women more than any other, or any group of men.'

Own Community

They approached Martin Lynch who had been writer-in-residence in the Lyric, because they knew he was interested in working with actors and they liked the approach in his plays to Belfast life. From a vague start with the desire for a show rooted in the history of Belfast women but not much information ('We were finding things out about our own city.'—Brenda) they narrowed it down to the two-week long York Street mill-girls' strike.

Marie Jones, who surprised herself with an unsuspected talent for writing dialogue, says research was the longest, hardest and most enjoyable part of preparation. 'Sadie

Patterson [veteran trade unionist] was our first contact and inspiration. She told us about her own life in the mills and she told us about the strike.'

Great Talkers

Hours of taped memories from great talkers are distilled into a script, part improvised, part written, part reported, with cuts suggested by director Pam Brighton. When the mainly female audience in the old Ardoyne mill went tense with emotion, and when they roared and laughed and cheered, they reacted to their own grannies talking, or so the cast like to think.

It makes for a lively show. Between them the five play a multitude of parts, Marie, for example, substituting a shiny serge jacket for her shawl to become Charlie, the anti-strike, anti-woman, know-all husband of Lizzie (Brenda) who worries endlessly what her Charlie will say as the strike goes on, or even worse, what Charlie's mother will say, not to mention her own dear departed: 'My mother used to say, get 'til your work and keep yourself 'til yourself. She always made sure you had a nice clean shawl ... As my Charlie says, leave it to the ones that knows best.'

What seem to be the production's chief virtues, the verve, for example, with which the women play men's parts, spring more from practice than principle, the performers maintain. 'We looked for actors in the beginning, but there were none unemployed long enough at the right time to qualify for the grant we got from Action for Community Employment (ACE),' Brenda maintained.

'In this town if you're male and you've two legs and you're not blind, you get the part,' she adds with a grin and a glint in her eye. So they played the parts themselves. 'I'm playing my da,' said Marie. 'They're the women's perceptions of the men we're playing,' Brenda adds. 'All the women we talked to, practically, they'd talk for hours about conditions at work, the hardship, the illnesses, and you'd have to ask them about their men. Then they'd say, "Oh, he beat me, or he drank".' Nonetheless, men love the play, they both insist.

Men Watching

'It's the first time for a lot of men watching women being witty and clever and sympathetic and strong, because very few plays present women like that. Certainly there's a message there—they have amazing spirit and resilience and they were exploited.'

Now they want to take the show further afield, to more places around the north, perhaps to England, Canada. 'For a long time people felt Belfast was a cultural desert and people from England came over to give us of their wisdom—now the situation in London's dire and we feel a certain commitment to Belfast, to force a recognition that there is a core of talent here.'

They face considerable difficulties, not least the problem of cash to tour, since neither Arts Council funds tours beyond its borders. But where there's life there's hope and life there certainly is. In the words of Charabanc's own (not modest) posters: ' ... discover the mills, face the poverty, shun the workhouse ... It will make you laugh; it will make you cry ... There is a charabanc going in your area soon ... '

If a Charabanc can't keep touring, what can?

Irish Times August 1984
prior to the production going on tour to Sligo and Limerick.

The Amazons from Belfast

Dr A Obraztsove

They did not ride up on horseback as befits Amazons. But their theatre's posters and programmes depict a huge open-topped motor, such as formerly existed for excursions. The new company is indeed called 'Charabanc Theatre Company'. It consists entirely of women—five actresses full of *joie de vivre*, radiant with smiles, given to loud laughter and to cracking witty, sometimes risqué jokes—Maureen Macauley, Eleanor Methven, Brenda Winter, Marie Jones and Carol Moore. They are still quite young but have acquired professional experience. And the play they put on at the Dublin Festival—*Lay Up Your Ends*—was light-hearted, optimistic and permeated with witticisms, although it might seem that neither the situation in their native city, as in Northern Ireland as a whole, nor the subject chosen for the play, nor their own experience of life, would at all predispose one to joy or mirth.

The decision to organise their own theatre came about two years ago after they had managed to obtain material backing.

Before that, each of the participants in the new venture had long and vainly sought to find work. The actress-enthusiasts invited a producer over from London—likewise a woman, Pam Brighton—and got in as artistic director, a man this time, Martin Lynch. All together, announcing that the charabanc was setting out on its 'first excursion—destination Belfast 1911, when the city shuddered with the noise of the looms and the humming of the spindles'—they put together their show, calling it *Lay Up Your Ends*.

It is very difficult to define the genre of this production. It is based on a complex balance of drama and comedy, tragedy and farce. In Belfast in 1911 the looms and the spindles fell silent for a time and the city was shaken by an unprecedented strike in the spinning mills; more than 2000 women took part in it, in revolt against inhuman working conditions, against oppression, against infant mortality etc. All this is discussed in the Charabanc Theatre Company's first work which touches on important social and political problems. Concentrating their audience's attention on social conflicts and social struggle, the creators of *Lay Up Your Ends* at the same time warn of the danger of inflaming religious confrontations. It is note-worthy that in the company itself there are both Catholic and Protestant actresses and they get on together splendidly. In a number of episodes in the production the question is raised of the alleged impossibility of normal co-existence between Catholics and Protestants and this point of view is satirised.

Drama and the theatre occupy a special place today in the artistic and social life of Northern Ireland. Very close links are emerging between politics and the stage. Martin Lynch, who has associated himself with Charabanc, came from politics to play-writing because he believed in the power of the theatre as a political forum. Explaining the general situation on the contemporary Irish stage, the author of a number of profound and passionate social dramas, Brian Friel, writes: 'Short stories affect each person individually; they are a face-to-face dialogue, an intimate conversation. But the playwright addresses not a single person but a group of people and he exists thanks to this group; this is no longer an intimate conversation but a public statement.'

But, in displaying its serious political spectacle to the Dubliners, the Belfast theatre sought to convince them that it had no intention of confining itself to stage propaganda methods. The roots of the Charabanc Theatre's art are in folklore traditions, in the bases of a popular culture which is capable of ridiculing everything and everyone in order to reveal the truth. Like other Irish productions, *Lay Up Your Ends* impressed by the bright vitality of its genre patterns and by the precision of its detail. Each performer created her own image, close to her individuality, of a Belfast mill-girl—historically specific, with her own temperament and peculiar inner world. However, in the course of the action the actresses had on a number of occasions to re-incarnate themselves in other personages, including the bosses of the mill; they had to put on male attire and make up appropriately.

One critic in his review of *Lay Up Your Ends*, stressing that this is at the same time a comic and a political spectacle, observed, addressing future audiences: 'It will make you laugh and it will make you cry.' The Charabanc Theatre Company's unexpected and multi-layered performance won acclaim from Dublin audiences as it did earlier from audiences in other Irish towns and villages where the bold, determined Belfast 'Amazons', with their faith in the future of Ireland and of the Irish Theatre, have contrived to perform.

This October the Charabanc visited the Soviet Union. Excerpts from *Lay Up Your Ends* shown on the stages of Moscow, Leningrad and Vilnius were warmly received by Soviet audiences also.

Sovetskaya Kultura, 30th October 1984

Kitty's Memories Inspire New Play

Pauline Reynolds

Ninety-year-old Kitty Irwin minds the time when 'a yard of cloth made you a coat', when the 'Queen's granny' passed over the bridge in a horse and carriage and the hit of the day was 'Mama dear, I want my Papa'.

Kitty is the stuff nostalgia is made of. A contented great-great-grandmother, she thoughtfully recounts her childhood memories of a hard day's graft in the linen mills with ease and precision.

This active Belfast pensioner who still enjoys a pinch of Gallagher Scent snuff, vividly remembers the 12-hour shifts at York St mill, walking barefoot from her Short Strand home to work and the great crack when the whistle blew sounding clocking-off time.

Kitty is one of the inspirations for a new play highlighting the lives of five mill workers during a strike in 1911. It recalls the sad times and the happy times, the struggles and the simple pleasures that a group of women experienced at the beginning of the century.

The play is the brain-child of five out-of-work actresses who got together to try to create a work of local interest in which they could all be involved. It was born initially out of frustration.

They felt that most plays were written by men, many geared towards men and saw their free time as an opportunity to research an era of history where women played a vital role—the linen industry.

The group have called themselves Charabanc Theatre Company and are writing the script with Belfast playwright, Martin Lynch. As yet the title is not finalised, but the suggestion—'Lay Up Your Ends', a mill phrase—is still under consideration.

Yesterday three of the actresses, Brenda Winter, Maureen Macauley and Eleanor Methven, visited Mrs Irwin's home in Short Strand's White Street to recapture her memories, thoughts and experiences on paper.

Mrs Irwin delights in recalling her past. Every date is etched in her mind and she has no trouble remembering her friends and colleagues from the mill and her youth.

One of her earliest recollections is of the time Queen Mary visited Belfast and it still brings a chuckle from the fine old lady who has spent all her life in Short Strand.

'I mind the time, I was only seven or eight and my mother and father were all dressed up. They said to me, "Now Kitty, we are going on a very particular message and I don't want you following." Well, I put on my gutties and followed them up to the station. The militia men were marching and I saw my father and mother standing in the crowd. I hid behind them and the next thing, I saw my brother in the parade. I was so excited I shouted, "Hey, Ma, there's our Thomas John!" That was me caught out. They had gone to see the Queen's granny and I wasn't allowed,' she laughed.

Kitty says that times were hard in those days but maintains that there is 'a lot of badness' now. At the age of 14 she earned nine shillings. Asked what that was able to buy, Kitty replied, 'Ach, sure I never broke it. It all went to my mother'.

She fondly recalls how her mother baked bread on an open griddle in the fireplace and the innocent childhood games of skipping and making toy shops 'from oul bits of delph'.

Her day started in the mill at 6 a.m. It was a barefoot walk in all types of weather and, although tired out when she arrived home at about seven that same evening, Kitty believes the young people then were far happier than those nowadays.

Her first husband died in 1916 at the Somme and, with tears in her eyes, she can even now visualise the messenger-boy delivering the ominous telegram to her door.

'It said, *Killed in action 1916, first of July, Battle of the Somme.*' She remarried, had three children and now has nine grandchildren, four great-grandchildren and one great-great-grandchild. Her husband died nineteen years ago.

Kitty is one of about 20 women who have helped in the theatre company's research. Together with fact-finding missions to the libraries and museums, they have gradually pieced together the basis of the play.

At present Martin Lynch is helping them finish it at the writers' paradise in Monaghan, the Tyrone Guthrie Centre, Annaghmakerrig.

Brenda explained the aims of their venture and their hopes for the future: 'This is not a feminist play but simply one outlining life during the peak of Belfast's booming linen-mill times. Our opening night is Sunday, May 15th, at the Arts Theatre. We hope to tour leisure centres in May, community centres in June and seaside resorts during the summer. The whole experience is filled with enthusiasm and commitment and has been marvellous for all of us,' she said.

The other two actresses involved in the drama are Carol Moore [Scanlan] and Marie [Sarah] Jones and the artistic director of the Hull Truck Community Theatre in England will direct the play.

Irish News, undated

Biographical Notes

MARTIN LYNCH co-wrote *Lay Up Your Ends* and was a director of Charabanc Theatre Company. He has had a long and very successful career as a playwright and is a keen community activist. He is currently developing his career into new areas of theatrical production.

MARIE JONES has worked extensively as an actress in TV, film and theatre but in recent years has become internationally renowned for her writing, most notably *Stones in his Pockets* which has been produced now in many countries around the world. She was a founder member of Charabanc and after *Lay Up Your Ends* became the principal writer for Charabanc productions. She is based in Belfast.

BRENDA WINTER was a founder member of Charabanc and afterwards the founder and first Artistic Director of REPLAY, Northern Ireland's theatre-in-education company. She combines a successful career as an actor, director and writer with the completion of a PhD at Queen's University (Belfast) on the life and work of the Ulster dramatist George Shiels.

MAUREEN MACAULEY trained as a dancer. She has worked with a wide range of companies as an actor and choreographer. She was a founder member of Charabanc. Currently she is much sought-after as a stage-manager, in particular for the theatre-in-education company REPLAY. She is based in Belfast.

CAROL MOORE [Scanlan] was a founder member of Charabanc. She has had a very successful career as an actor and director. Since her time at Charabanc she has been notable for her energy in devising and developing her own projects and is currently starting a successful new career as a film-maker. She is based in Belfast.

ELEANOR METHVEN was a founder member of Charabanc. Along with Carol Moore, she remained with Charabanc throughout its existence. She has since had a very successful career as a TV, film and theatre actor working throughout Ireland. She is based in Dublin.

PAM BRIGHTON has had a distinguished career as a theatre director with a number of groundbreaking companies. She directed *Lay Up Your Ends* and a number of other Charabanc productions. Later she became a drama producer with the BBC in Belfast and Artistic Director of Dubbeljoint Theatre Co.

DAI JENKINS played Leadpipe and provided the musical direction for the first production. He has since returned to his native Wales.

AIDAN McCANN took over the role of Leadpipe and with Dai Jenkins became the 'forgotten men' of the production.

UNA WALKER was the set designer on the original production. She was awarded a PhD at the University of Ulster in 2008. Today the main focus of her work is site-specific installations.

IAN McELHINNEY was the producer of *Lay Up Your Ends* and a director of the company. He is a very successful TV, film and theatre actor and director working extensively in Ireland and Great Britain but continues to make Belfast his base.

CHERRIE McILWAINE was one of the three company directors who at a necessary time acted as a financial guarantor for Charabanc. She is now a very familiar voice to audiences of BBC Radio Ulster.